W9-BSC-810

# The Morning Comes and Also the Night

# The Morning Comes and Also the Night

Byron MacDonald

Copyright © 2001 by Byron MacDonald.

Library of Congress Number:     2001116787
ISBN #:          Hardcover        978-0-7388-6919-3
                 Softcover        978-0-7388-6920-9

All rights reserved. No part of this book may be reproduced or
transmitted in any form or by any means, electronic or mechanical,
including photocopying, recording, or by any information storage
and retrieval system, without permission in writing from the
copyright owner.

This book was printed in the United States of America.

**To order additional copies of this book, contact:**
Xlibris Corporation
1-888-795-4274
www.Xlibris.com
Orders@Xlibris.com

# Contents

THIS BOOK IS DEDICATED TO THE MINISTRIES OF THE LORD JESUS CHRIST AT ROLLING HILLS COVENANT CHURCH. I AM INCREDIBLY THANKFUL FOR THE TREMENDOUS SUPPORT AND EFFORTS OF MANY AT THE CHURCH ON BEHALF OF THIS PROJECT. I AM PARTICULARLY GRATEFUL FOR THE HELP OF MY ASSISTANT, THERESA COCHRAN, AND FOR MY LIFE PARTNER, LYNDA.

# Introduction

"Watchman, what of the night?
Watchman, what of the night?"

The watchman said, "The morning comes, and also the
night.
*If you will inquire, inquire; Return! Come back!*"
Isaiah 21:11-12

Did you ever wonder what it would be like to live as part of biblical times, and to have your life as part of the story? Wonder no more. You are. In all of the Bible the most talked about generation is not that of Moses or Joshua or even the Lord Jesus, the most talked about generation is the generation alive at the return of the Lord Jesus Christ. An enormous amount of the Bible is written just to that generation. It is true that application of the teaching applies to many issues between the first and Second Coming of Jesus, but the focus is the last generation, our generation. This book will share the biblical and historical reason for such a statement to be made and why it is obvious that Jesus wants us to know the generation of His return. We will explore not only why Jesus wants us to know, but what He wants us to do in response. We each have the opportunity to choose our place in the biblical history by our responses.

In Old Testament walled cities, the watchman bore an important responsibility. While the people of the city slept, it was the watchman's responsibility to stay awake and keep watch on the city walls. He would watch for the danger of approaching enemies. He would watch for internal dangers, such as an outbreak of fire. The watchman's responsibility was to warn the city of danger and mobilize them for response.

As the watchman of Isaiah 21:11,12 keeps watch, someone asks him, *"Watchman, what of the night?"* It was a typical question. The hoped for answer was, "All is well." As the watchman answers back, though, he gives a response that seems a contradiction. The watchman reports signs indicating both morning and night are coming. How could the watchman be looking at the same signs and see both the coming of dawn and the coming of night? Yet the answer to that question, is the same answer which causes us to look to our world and see the evidence in the Bible and current affairs that reaches the same conclusion. The morning comes and also the night.

As we will look at the fulfillment of signs from the Bible in our generation, they tell us, *"Morning is coming!"* The promise of Jesus that one day He will return and take the church home as His bride is about to be fulfilled. What has been the blessed hope of the Christian since Jesus left, is now about to happen. We are told in 2 Peter 1:19, *"And so we have the prophetic word confirmed, which you do well to heed as a light that shines in a dark place, until the day dawns and the morning star arises in your hearts"*; The long time of living in what C. S. Lewis calls the "Shadowlands" is about over. Any moment now, Jesus will come back with those who have passed through death as believers in Christ, and resurrect His church, and take her home as His bride. *"Watchman, what of the night? . . . The morning comes . . ."*

The watchman also said the same signs indicate night is coming. The Day of the Lord is about to happen. It is a day of darkness. It is a day of judgment. God is about to judge this world. The warning signs of the coming of judgment are all around us. The same signs that indicate Jesus will soon take His church home, also indicate that the Tribulation and seven years of increasing horrors and the reality of God's judgment are about to come. We will see why God wants us to take the warnings of the judgments of Revelation with great seriousness. Revelation is not fairy tales. It is deadly serious history about to happen.

I remember after the fall of the Soviet Empire, and the establishment of many independent republics in what was once the Soviet Union, an interview of a justice in the equivalent of the Russian Supreme Court. The interviewer noted a painting prominently displayed in the office of the justice. It was a painting of the vast Russian heartland. The painting was done in faint light with the sun just below the horizon. After studying the picture for a while the interviewer was puzzled. Does the painting portray the coming of dawn, and a picture of the hope of the rising sun? Or, does the picture portray a setting sun, and the warning of the coming of night? The Russian justice proposed that one couldn't tell from the picture. It was his same feeling about the future of Russia. As he looked at the signs of Russian history, he could not tell what they indicated for Russia's future. As we consider what the signs of the Bible indicate about the future, there is no uncertainty as to their meaning. They indicate both the coming of morning for those in Christ, and the coming of the night of judgment for those who are outside of faith in Him.

Perhaps what will be of greatest controversy as one reads this book, is the identification of the United States of America as the commercial Babylon of Revelation 18. I believe as you consider the biblical evidence, and see what is happening through the USA in the world, you will come to the same sickening conclusion. You will take a step back at the fury God has toward this nation. You will be sobered by the reasons for her judgment. You will be forced to consider what it means when God says in Revelation 18:4, *"Come out of her, my people, lest you share in her sins and lest you receive of her plagues."* You will see why an America that has reduced the issues of national life down to one, "It's the economy," and has persuaded the leaders of the world that is what matters, perfectly fulfills the driving force that seduces the world. A country that has done so much good, in fact has been key to the Gospel going to the ends of the earth, is accused by God of having misled the world. As the accusation says in Revelation 18:23, *"For your merchants were the great men of the earth, for by your sorcery all the nations were deceived."* You will see why a strong USA economy, leading the global economy, and a weakened American Presidency, perfectly fit the scenario of the Tribulation scene.

As I write I know that there are many people who love the Lord Jesus and who love the Word of God, as much as I, who will disagree with what I say. I understand and accept it. Prophecy is the most challenging part of the Bible to understand. That people disagree with me is not a test of theirs or my orthodoxy, understanding of the Bible, or ability as students. Having said this, however, I also must state that what I write I offer without hesitation as what the Bible teaches. I believe this part of the Bible has been given us to understand, particularly as we live in the dawn of its fulfillment. I write with a conviction that if one lets the Bible speak, it does so clearly, with understanding, and without ambiguity. God wants us to know, understand, and respond, and we can. This is not rocket science, this is the Word of God given to us with the Holy Spirit, and it is for us to understand and to respond.

You should also know I write as a preacher. I write to persuade you, not only as to what it says, but as to who you should be and what you should do in light of what it says. I offer this not from the intellectuals dispassionate distance. I offer this not as the teacher content to explain. I offer it not as a debate with others. I offer it with the passion of a watchman, who sees the danger and the opportunity, who loves and cares about people, and who cries out with God, *"Return! Come back!"* The watchman who cries out, *"I must do the works of Him who sent Me while it is day; the night is coming when no one can work."* John 9:5. I write with the passion of the watchman who says with Peter in 2 Peter 3:11-13, *"Therefore, since all these things will be dissolved, what manner of people ought you to be in holiness and godliness, looking for and hastening the coming day of God, because of which the heavens will be dissolved, being on fire, and the elements will melt with fervent heat? Nevertheless we, according to His promise, look for new heavens and a new earth in which righteousness dwells.* " I write with the passion of Revelation that ends with, *"even so, come, Lord Jesus!"* I want this book to be used of God to change your life.

As you read, I pray this book motivates you to see your life purified and ready for the return of the Lord Jesus Christ, and that it motivates you to maximize this moment for the Gospel in your community, nation, and world.

So, did you ever wonder what it would be like to live in biblical times and have your life as part of the story? Well, you are. Let's see why this statement is true and where you are or can be in the story.

# 1 | The End Is the Beginning

*"Remember the former things of old, for I am God, and*
*there is no other; I am God, and there is none like Me,*
*Declaring the end from the beginning, and from ancient*
*times things that are not yet done, saying 'My counsel*
*shall stand, and I will do all my pleasure.'"*
Isaiah 46:9,10

So, how does the world end? In an ecological nightmare as the balance of the natural world is broken beyond repair? In a series of terrorists and rogue nations starting a nuclear night from which the world never awakes? A meltdown of computer systems that revert man back to a stone age? How does the world end? And, what will happen to you when it does? Politicians in the USA like to say that all politics are local. Voters really vote on local issues, more than national or international. Well, this book has the point of view that all Bible prophecy is personal. It's about you and me.

What if I were to tell you the world as we know it is about to end, would you be interested? What if I were to relate it all to you and your life, nothing extra or wasted, would you want to read more? I can promise you this because you are living right in the middle of some of the most important parts of history which the Bible describes. I want to show you some things so much out of the Bible and out of the newspaper that you will never quite read the Bible or the newspaper the same. I want to show you things that I pray will change your life. I want to show you things that help you decide how one key part of the last chapter of the Bible history ends. The part of the Bible's history that is about you.

I can promise you this, because God cares about you. He has already decided how the world is going to end, and He wants you to know. As He says in Isaiah 46:10, He has already declared the end from the beginning. But the part of the end still having one of two endings, is your part. The Bible says the end of the world as we know it, will really be the beginning of eternity as God will have it. An eternity in which heaven will be on earth. An eternity so wonderful the Bible struggles to find words spectacular enough to describe it. An eternity, though, that will find most people not part of it, sharing a fate that the Bible struggles to find words grave enough to describe what it will be like. So, it really is an important subject to understand.

The Bible has a lot to say about one generation in particular (a generation in the Bible seems to be approximately 40 years). It is the generation that will see everything come to an end, an end that will really be the new beginning. What makes this 40-year period of time interesting is that I believe we are in it, and that there isn't much time left.

I want to describe some things that Jesus and the Bible say will be true of this last generation so that you will see how important it is to know this information. I am absolutely convinced that the Lord Jesus wants you to know you are in it, and that time is short, so that you can make the best decisions with your life right now. Jesus says in Luke 21:31-32, *"So you also, when you see these things happening, know that the kingdom of God is near. Assuredly, I say to you, this generation will by no means pass away till all these things take place."* The key thoughts here are two. There are some things we can see happening that will identify the last generation. The generation will not pass away until it is all done.

Before we get into the details of this last generation in the chapters to follow, let me give you the scenario of the world as the end that brings the beginning comes. The world that is as much a part of today's newspapers as it is the books of the Bible written from almost 2,000 to 3,400 years ago. Remember all of this is possible because there is a God who says He declares the end from the beginning. I'm not sure how all that works, but I do believe Him, and I pray you do and will, as well.

The key event the Bible says will be true is that we will see the nation of Israel once again among the nations of the world. We will see them take Jerusalem as their capital. We will see the world leaders desperately trying to figure out how to make peace with her and her neighbors, as it will be key to peace for the world. This will be the key, unmistakable sign that this is the last generation, the end, just before the beginning of eternity. And, of course, Israel was reestablished as a nation in 1948, and it did take Jerusalem as its capital in 1967. The only generation since 585 BC to see the nation of Israel among the nations of the world, with Jerusalem as its capital is ours, you and me.

The Bible says we will see a developing political and economic union of nations in Europe that roughly parallels the old Roman Empire. We will see at the beginning no strong leader, but just a group of nations combining together. And of course that is happening as the United States of Europe establishes the Euro Dollar. Many believe the Euro Dollar will become the standard for the world, replacing the USA dollar.

The Bible says we will see one nation whose merchants will dominate the world's economies, and who will live in luxury as compared to the rest of the world. This nation's merchants will work with the world leaders to convince that it is a global economy, and that they need to let this nation be the queen of the world's economy. This nation's merchants will seduce the leaders and merchants of the world with their business, and will be a key part in establishing a foundation for a one world government. This nation will convince the world the only issue which matters is the economy. Of course it will only be a scheme to keep the select merchants rich, and this nation living in luxury, but it will convince the merchants and political leaders of the world. Because in its riches, many of them will get rich. That this nation the Bible describes only matches the USA, is one of the most disturbing parts of the scenario. It amazes me that more Bible students don't see that. But as this book is really for you, I want to show you the evidence that I hope convinces you.

The Bible also talks about this generation's rapidly increasing knowledge. As we now know man's knowledge doubles in less than two years, all knowledge man has acquired in the time up to 1996, has now doubled in the time period since. The Bible also talks about international travel, as people rush about the globe. It talks about intensifying storms and other natural disasters. It talks about famines, and diseases taking lives. It talks about wars and violence. In short, it talks about the world described for us in the multiplying news channels that bombard us with its reports twenty-four hours a day, seven days a week. We become so accustomed to it that a report that 10% of North Korea's population has died of famine in the last few years hardly even raises an eyebrow.

So, are you interested? Do you want to know how a Book completed nineteen hundred years ago, written over a period of thirty three-hundred years has so much to say about today? Very simple, there is a God, and He wants you to know. There is a God who not only calls Himself the Beginning, but also calls Himself the End. There is a God who not only calls Himself the First, but also calls Himself the Last. He has a message for you. Let's lay out the future as God describes it and see where we are right now in relation to it.

# 2 | The Times They Are

## A'Changin

*"Blow the trumpet in Zion, and sound an alarm in My*
*holy mountain! Let all the inhabitants of the land tremble;*
*for the day of the Lord is coming for it is at hand: A day of*
*darkness and gloominess, a day of clouds and thick dark-*
*ness, like the morning clouds spread over the mountains."*
Joel 2:1-2a

I came to adulthood during the
1960's. The 60's were times of enormous change, from which the
world never has recovered. A song that came to define the time
period was by Bob Dylan. The song was "The Times They Are
A'Changin." As I look at the world today, as we enter a new millennium, there are signs of times changing as never before. All
of us have a sense that something is happening that is different
from anything we have seen before. Some call it a kind of
millennial fever that strikes the world when a new millennium
comes. But I think inside, we know, this is different. Weather in
chaos, oceans in turmoil, the world being drawn closer together,
and yet no one can figure if it is good or bad. One moment the
world rides a wave of euphoria over the economic boom spreading around the world, and the next moment in fear that the Asian,

Russian, and South American economic crisis might plunge us all into a tailspin that ends in recession, or worse a depression.

Well, I have some good and bad news for you. The times they are a'changin but not by the hand of man, it is by the hand of God. To an amazing degree in our thinking we have developed either an evolutionary view of time, or an Eastern religious view of time. To some, applying an evolutionary model to mankind, we are evolving upwards. Some see the new millennium as a strategic moment for us to collectively apply the power of our thoughts to enable mankind to evolve into a new age, a new order. The bumper stickers call us to "Think Peace." Some applying Eastern religious thought believe life is a circle. We are in an endless cycle, but it is possible for us to enter a new cycle, to progress. The Bible states, in contrast, that history is not evolving, or being run in cycles, but it is moving toward one grand moment. The grand moment of God's plan to bring His order to the world.

The Bible teaches that what is next in God's plan is something called the Day of the Lord. The Day of the Lord is a constant theme in both the Old and New Testament. It is a Day that will bring to mankind and the nations of the world, the judgment of God and the reward of God. That's why its coming is both good news and bad news. It is why I have told you that there is a part of this story still being written, and that is your part. For the Day of the Lord is about the Lord Jesus and God's plan for the world through Him. This is a very important and urgent issue, for all around us the signs that the seasons of God's dealing with mankind are changing. I think time before the coming Day of the Lord is very short.

Before we see the change of the seasons of God's dealing with man, and the coming Day of the Lord, let's see what season we are in now. Currently we are in what could be called the Age of Grace. It began with the coming to live amongst us of God Himself, by His Son, the Lord Jesus Christ. Jesus came because mankind was in a terrible state. We were created by God and for

God, but we had rebelled against Him. Each one of us had done our own thing. The Bible calls that sin, or to miss the mark. It says of all us in Romans 3:23, *"For all have sinned and fall short of the glory of God."* The glory of God is what we were created for. You and I were made in the likeness of God, so we might know Him, enjoy Him, and bring Him the glory (importance) that He deserves over all the earth. But, instead, we have each done our own things. We have missed the mark. We have fallen terribly short.

Because we have fallen short, missed the mark, God has called us to live by, it leaves us in a tragic situation we can't change on our own. The Bible goes on to say in Romans 6:23, *"For the wages of sin is death, but the gift of God is eternal life in Christ Jesus our Lord."* Our sins have accumulated to us a debt with God. God is the Judge, and He makes us accountable to Him. Our sins have accumulated a debt we can't pay off, either in this life or in the life to come. Death often means something different in the Bible than we think. When we use death, we refer to the death of our body. The Bible uses death that way sometimes as well. But the most powerful and frequent use of the word death is in contrast to God. God is life. Death is to be separated from God. Our problem with death goes all the way back to the beginning with Adam and Eve. When they disobeyed God, they were cut off from God. Because we are all from Adam, and in his likeness, we have his condition.

I remember watching a movie about a condemned man on death row. In the movie as he is being taken to the gas chamber, the guard goes ahead saying, "Dead man walking." It seems a cruel reminder to someone so soon to die, but there is a real way it describes all of us. We are each "Dead man/woman walking." It's why life so often doesn't work the way we want it to work. We were made for God, and without Him at the center of our lives the most important part is missing.

The problem though gets worse when our life on this earth ends. For when physical death comes, it doesn't end our life, we just change locations. When it says, *"The wages of sin is death,"* it means our sins earn us separation from God not only now, but forever. The wages for our sin is the judgment of God, and there is nothing we can do in this life, or the one to come, that can pay off our debts. Good works can't do it, being religious can't do it. Being baptized in the church won't do it. Not even going to hell and suffering for a while will do it. There is nothing we can do.

The Good News is that what we can't do, God has done for us through Jesus. It says, *"The gift of God is eternal life in Christ Jesus our Lord."* Romans 6:23. You see the words "eternal life?" Those words are in contrast to death. Eternal life means life forever connected to God as part of His kingdom. It's not called eternal death in the verse, because we each have a chance to receive the gift of eternal life. As long as we have breath it's not over for us. I suppose it has happened that someone walking to the gas chamber, a dead man walking, has gotten a last moment reprieve. That is what is possible for you, for me. We can go from a dead man/woman walking, to those who have eternal life. How does that happen? The Bible says it is a gift in Christ Jesus our Lord. Let's see how to have that gift in Jesus. It's the most important truth to respond to we could ever hear.

My father used to tell me that if something is too good to be true, it is most likely too good to be true. What the Bible has to say, though, while seeming to be too good to be true, is actually truth itself. Truth you can put your whole life into. The Bible says in Romans 10:9,10,13 how to have this gift, *"That if you confess with your mouth the Lord Jesus and believe in your heart that God raised Him from the dead, you will be saved. For with the heart one believes unto righteousness, and with the mouth confession is made unto salvation . . . . For whoever calls on the name of the Lord shall be saved."*

There are two important parts of having this free gift from God of eternal life, living forever with Him and not being judged in hell. One part is to let Jesus change the whole direction of your life. The word, "confess," means to say the same thing as. The Bible says to confess with your mouth the Lord Jesus. The name Jesus means savior. Lord means boss, ruler, the One in charge. If sin is doing our own thing, which is the problem, turning your life over to Jesus to be your boss is the opposite. The Bible calls this repentance. Repentance means a 180-degree turnaround. Repentance doesn't just mean being sorry, or wanting to change. To repent is to turn it all around. You make the choice to have Jesus be the boss of your life.

The other part is to believe that God has raised Jesus from the dead. The Bible teaches that Jesus died for a purpose. He is God Who became man. But He was sent by God, the Father, to live among us, and then to die for us. Jesus died in judgment. He died in judgment for our sins. He paid the debt. The wages of sin is death in judgment, so Jesus took our place in judgment. The debt that couldn't be paid, He paid for us.

But our verse says, believe in your heart that God raised Him from the dead. Jesus didn't stay dead. He rose back to life on the third day after He died. He rose again in a body, showing He conquered death, sin, and Satan. The Ressurection is the proof that Jesus is the One. Romans 1:4 says about Jesus and the Ressurection, *"and declared to be the Son of God with power according to the Spirit of holiness, by the resurrection from the dead."* God raised Jesus back to life by the power of the Holy Spirit because Jesus is the One to save us.

To believe in your heart that God raised Him from the dead is to believe that He died as a substitute for your sins, that He rose in triumph, and that if I trust Him He will give me eternal life. What a deal! We stop wasting our life, come to Jesus, give Him our sins, start following Him, and He saves us and gives us eternal life. Eternal life means forever I will be right with God. When death comes He will take me to be with Him. When judgment comes I will never face it, for He paid for all my sins already. No wonder the Bible keeps calling this Good News (the Gospel).

Now who is this for, who can be saved? The Bible says whoever calls on the Name of the Lord will be saved. This means you and me. It means we each can do this, for God promised that whoever wants to can come. It's just a simple prayer that is placed at the end of this book. If you pray and believe in your heart, and turn to follow Jesus, you will have it, eternal life. It's a gift. It's your chance to say how the story for you will end.

As we go back to the question of what season we are in now, we are in the season when God wants this message of the free gift of salvation to go to everyone in the world. This season is often called "The Age of Grace." Grace refers to the offer of the free gift of salvation. Romans 1:5-6 says it this way, *"Through Him (Jesus) we have received grace and apostleship for obedience to the faith among all nations in His (Jesus) name."* The purpose that God has for this season in His dealings with mankind is telling everyone about the opportunity of the free gift. God doesn't want anybody to have to face judgment and to go to hell. 2 Peter 3:9 says about God that He, *". . . is longsuffering toward us, not willing that any should perish but that all should come to repentance."* What a great and awesome God who is so good, and so patient. He has let this go on a long time since Jesus, almost 2,000 years.

The Bible says though there is a day when God will say "enough." The seasons will change, and they will change so dramatically it stretches the imagination to picture it. This new season will be called the Day of the Lord. It is a day of judgment and a day of reward. As we picture this, I am going to stick for a while with the Old Testament book of Joel. I'll share the passages from the Bible so you can keep reading the book uninterrupted.

The Bible says the day of Grace ends and the Day of the Lord comes. When it comes it comes as a day of darkness, a day of terror, a day of judgment. When will this day be and what will it be like? When this day will be Jesus promised would be easy to recognize. As the seasons change, the signs of the changing season will be easy to see.

The Bible says in Joel 3:1,2, *"For behold, in those days and at that time, when I bring back the captives of Judah and Jerusalem, I will also gather all nations, and bring them down to the valley of Jehosaphat; and I will enter into judgment with them there on account of My people, My heritage of Israel, whom they have scattered among the nations."* The valley of judgment described here is what is later described in the book of Revelation as Armageddon. The valley, located in Northern Israel, stretches from the Jordan River to the Mediterranean Sea. Notice what it says. When I bring back the captives of Judah and Jerusalem, I will also gather all nations into the valley of what will be the Lord's judgment.

What is the sign the seasons are about to change? It is a sign that only we in the second half of the 20th and beginning of the 21st centuries have seen. It is the sign of the restoration of Israel as a nation among the nations of the world. This has not happened since 585 years before Jesus was born. Yet it has happened now. In 1948 after the ashes of the gas ovens of World War ll, one of the great miracles in all of history occurred. By the action of the United Nations Israel was established as a nation. In 1967 in another providential act of God in history, Israel gained full control of Jerusalem and named it as their capital. As we will later see in the words of Jesus, this is the key sign that the season is about to change. The key sign that the Day of Grace will soon end, and the Day of the Lord will begin.

We will spend a whole chapter on the significance of Israel in God's plan, but the key for us now is that Joel says when we see this happen, we should know the terrifying Day of the Lord is about to come. Let me give you just a little taste from Revelation of what part of that day will be like. It says in Revelation 6:12-17, *"I looked and when He opened the sixth seal, and behold, there was a great earthquake; and the sun became black as sackcloth of hair, and the moon became like blood. And the stars of heaven fell to the earth, as a fig tree drops its late figs when it is shaken by a mighty wind. Then the sky receded as a scroll when it is rolled up, and every mountain and island was moved out of its place. And the kings of the earth, the great men, the rich men, the commanders, the mighty men, every slave and every free man, hid themselves in the caves and in the rocks of the mountains, and said to the mountains and rocks, "Fall on us and hide us from the face of Him who sits on the throne and from the wrath of the Lamb! For the great day of His wrath has come, and who is able to stand?"*

Sobering, isn't it. An earthquake so big every mountain and island moves. A cloud of dust and smoke so huge the sun appears dark, and the moon a blood red. Stars of heaven, meteors hitting the atmosphere. People so terrified they would rather die than face it. It is called the Day of the Wrath of God and the Lamb. The Lamb is Jesus. No longer are the arms of God reaching out in love and calling us to Jesus. They are now closed in judgment. We see Jesus now with the wrath of God bringing judgment on the peoples and nations of earth because they have rejected Him. How tragic it would be that day to wake up to the truth of Jesus and find it is too late. That is why it is so important to make a choice for Jesus today.

# 3 | Can You Really Know the Future?

*"Surely the Lord God does nothing, Unless He reveals His secret to His servants the prophets."*
Amos 3:7

The election of 1998 in the USA again proves how difficult it is to predict the future when you are dealing with people. After all the scientific polling, all the analysis by the political experts, no one was close to predicting what really happened. Can you really know the future, and how does that work? People have been forever seeking for ways to discern the future. Every daily newspaper contains the horoscope section, where people supposedly can plot the future by the alignment of the stars and planets. Some people go to palm readers, psychic hotlines, tea leaves, tarot card readers. Yet all seem to be little more than guesses. The Bible though is unique. Not only is the Bible one of the sources that claims to know the future, it is the only one that has been proven to be 100 percent accurate in every prediction it has made that has been fulfilled so far. A little later we will look at the amazing accuracy with which the Bible predicted key events in the first coming to earth of the Lord Jesus. It is one of the powerful affirmations to us that Jesus truly is the One who God promised would come to save us from our sin, and bring us into the kingdom of God. But let's think about what makes predicting the future by the Bible possible.

The most important reason to know that the Bible can predict the future is because God is the One who led and enabled its writing. The Bible is the unique Book of all books, because it claims to be written by the Spirit of God. The Bible says in 2 Peter 1:19-21, *"And so we have the prophetic word confirmed, which you do well to heed as a light that shines in a dark place, until the day dawns and the morning star rises in your hearts; knowing this first, that no prophecy of Scripture is of any private interpretation, for prophecy never came by the will of man, but holy men of God spoke as they were moved by the Holy Spirit."* Do you see the picture? We live in darkness with no light of ultimate truth to us, only the opinions of one another. But the Bible is the light to our darkness, for it is the voice of God to us. Though it was written by human authors it says they were moved or carried along by the Spirit of God, so that they wrote God's Words, not theirs. 2 Timothy 3:16, another part of the Bible, says *"God breathed"* through them, and the result was the Word of God.

As it comes to the future, the Bible wants us to have such confidence in what God has said will happen, that it warns us not to mess with it. In Revelation 22:18-19, just about the last word before the Bible ends, it says, *"For I testify to everyone who hears the words of the prophecy of this book; If anyone adds to these things, God will add to him the plagues that are written in this book; and if anyone takes away from the words of the book of this prophecy, God shall take away his part from the Book of Life, from the holy city, and from the things which are written in this book."* That is very serious stuff, if you know anything about the terrible things Revelation says will happen. If you mess with the Bible and take away words, or add words, you will face the judgment of God. That is how seriously God wants us to take this book. It also provides a key to understanding it. God has brought His purpose to every word, not just the ideas. It is very important to understand this, if you are going to understand its predictions correctly.

Thus, we can understand the future because we have a Book that God has given us that reveals His truth and message to us. In the Bible it says the future can be predicted because God's hand is working in the affairs of this world to accomplish His purposes. It says that what God has decided to happen, how it will end, is how it *will* happen! The Bible says in Isaiah 46:9,11, *"Remember the former things of old, for I am God, and there is no other; I am God and there is none like Me, Declaring the end from the beginning, and from ancient times things that are not yet done, saying, 'My counsel shall stand, and I will do all My pleasure. Calling a bird of prey from the east, the man who executes My counsel from a far country. Indeed, I have spoken it; I will also bring it to pass. I have purposed it; I will also do it."* Very impressive statements aren't they? Here is God saying He determines the end from the beginning. He will predict from ancient times what will happen today in modern times. He is able to cause His will to be done.

So, what's His track record? The Bible claims to be the Word of God. The God of the Bible claims to be able to determine what happens in modern times with its predictions made in ancient times. Those are pretty amazing statements. How well does the Bible do in its predictions? We have already a huge accumulation of data to evaluate the claim. The Bible made 61 major prophecies about the first coming to earth of the Messiah, the Lord Jesus. Of these 61, every single one was fulfilled exactly. It is one of those amazing reasons we have to believe Jesus is the One. No one by chance could fulfill these 61. The odds of one person even fulling eight is one in ten to the seventeenth power. The odds of one person fulfilling 48 are one in ten to the one hundred fifty seventh power. That is a number all but unable to be calculated, and my math isn't good enough to calculate the full odds on one person fulfilling all 61.

The events of Jesus life predicted and fulfilled go from His conception, birth, ministry, death, and Ressurection. Many of these you are familiar with, such as His Virgin conception and Birth. The family of His birth. That Kings would bring gifts. That He would come out of Egypt. That He would do miracles. That He would die with criminals, and yet be buried with the rich. That He would have His hands and feet pierced, but no bones would be broken. That they would cast lots for His cloths, and on and on the list goes. The track record of the Bible predicting the future, in everything it has said so far, is perfect.

Let me give you one example. Zechariah is a book in the Bible written more than four hundred years before Jesus was born among us. We have found copies of this book in a Greek translation more than two hundred years before Jesus was born. So we know no one could have added this in later as a plot to fool us. I say that because its prophecy was so amazing and exact you would wonder how it could have predicted it so many years ago. In the prophecy it predicts that Jesus will be betrayed and how much they will give the person who betrays Him and what the person will do with the money. It is in Zechariah 11:12-13, *"Then I said to them, "If it is agreeable to you, give me my wages and if not refrain." So they weighed out for my wages thirty pieces of silver. And the Lord said to me, "Throw it to the potter"—that princely price they set on me. So I took the thirty pieces of silver and threw them into the house of the Lord for the potter."*

Did you get all that? The price of Jesus' betrayal would be thirty pieces of silver. The money would be thrown into the temple, the House of the Lord, yet it would go to the potter. Very specific and yet a combination of events absolutely unlikely to happen by chance. Let's see how close it came to the prediction when it did happen. Let's read from Matthew 27:3-7, *"Then Judas, His betrayer, seeing that He had been condemned, was remorseful and brought back the thirty pieces of silver to the chief priests and elders, saying, "I have sinned by betraying innocent blood." And they said, "What is that to us? You see to it!" Then he threw down the pieces of silver into the temple and departed, and went and hanged himself. But the chief priests took the silver pieces and said, "It's not lawful to put them into the treasury, because they are the price of blood." And they consulted together and bought with them the potter's field, to bury strangers in."*

Wow, that is so impressive. Exactly as predicted more than four hundred years before, is exactly how it happened. That it would be exactly thirty pieces of silver that Judas would be paid for betraying Jesus, and it was exactly thirty pieces of silver. That he wouldn't keep the money but throw it into the house of the Lord, the temple, and it is exactly what Judas did. That they wouldn't keep the money in the house of the Lord, but they would give it to the potter. Amazing, the potter! And they did. They bought a field owned by the potter to bury strangers in it. How could Zechariah know all that more than four hundred years before? Because there is a God, and He has declared the end from the beginning. And because there is a God who wants you to believe in Him through Jesus and to be saved from the coming judgment that all without faith in Jesus will face.

So, how can we know the future? The Bible has predicted it. The Bible reveals a God who has a plan, and whose plan will come to pass. Everything the Bible has predicted in the past that has been fulfilled was fulfilled exactly. Thus, we can have that same confidence about the future. Ready to learn more about the future it predicted you are living in right now? As we do, we first need to look at the key player among the nations and its importance to us in understanding. That is the nation of Israel, and God's amazing focus on it.

# 4 | The Seven-Year Plan

*"Seventy weeks are determined For your people and for
your holy city, To finish the transgression, To make an end
of sins, To make reconciliation for iniquity, To bring in
everlasting righteousness, To seal up vision and prophecy,
And to anoint the Most Holy."*

Daniel 9:24

Ever heard of words like 'The
Tribulation', 'The Apocalypse', the 'Antichrist', 'Armageddon'?
They all come from the Bible and they all concern one seven-year period of time that is the key to God's plan to bring history to
its grand conclusion. You know how history ends don't you? It
ends with the Lord Jesus Christ crowned as King of Kings, and
Lord of Lords. It ends with every knee bowing before Him and
declaring Him Lord. That is why it is so important that Jesus is
your Lord and Savior now. The Bible says that Jesus comes back
to end a seven-year period of time called the Tribulation (tribulation means trouble, stress, pressure). To understand it let's go
back with Daniel to a time when God revealed to him the future.

God loves Daniel a lot. He was a Jewish teenager in Jerusalem when he was taken a captive by the most powerful kingdom
of that day, Babylon. He was taken captive because the generations of Israel before him had been unfaithful to God. Time and
again they had rebelled, and finally God had said, 'Enough!'.
Israel was down to two tribes at that time. The other ten had been

taken captive long before. But now, even the last two, Judah and Benjamin, had gone too far in rebellion against God. What is significant about this is that this was the last time Israel was a nation among the nations before the second half of the 20th century. Isn't that significant? There hadn't been a nation of Israel among the nations of the world for more than 2,500 years until this generation we are living in now.

As Daniel was in captivity, he was seeking God for His future plans. He knew Jeremiah had said that they would be captive for 70 years. So, obviously, Daniel is counting the years and wondering what God is going to do in the future. As I said, God loves Daniel very much. In fact the angel told him he was highly respected in heaven. Quite a statement to have made about you. God so loved Daniel that He revealed to him not only the immediate future of Israel, but the future end of all history. God told Daniel that it would all be contained in a 490-year period of time. Let's see what God said, and understand the missing seven-year period of time.

As Daniel was seeking God for information on the future, the angel Gabriel appeared to Daniel. Sometimes angels, who are spiritual beings, can take on a human form. Gabriel told Daniel about a 490-year period of time. As you read this, Gabriel uses weeks instead of years. But later in the book it defines a week as seven 360 day years on the Jewish calendar. The Jewish calendar is a lunar calendar, a period of twelve lunar months. Listen to what Gabriel reveals from God. It's from Daniel 9:24-27. *"Seventy weeks are determined for your people, and for your holy city, to finish the transgression, to make an end of sins, to make reconciliation for iniquity, to bring in everlasting righteousness, to seal up vision and prophecy, and to anoint the Most Holy. Know therefore and understand, that from the going forth of the command to restore and build Jerusalem until Messiah the Prince, there shall be seven weeks and sixty two weeks; the street shall be built again, and the wall, even in troubled times. And after the sixty-two weeks Messiah shall be cut off, but not for Himself. And the people of the prince who is to come shall destroy the city and the sanctuary. The end of it shall be with a flood, and till the end of the war desolations are determined. Then he shall confirm a covenant with many for one week, but in the middle of the week he shall bring an end to sacrifice and offering. And on the wing of abomination shall be one who makes desolate, even until the consummation, which is determined, is poured out on the desolate."*

Did you get that? It's a lot, so let's break it down, because it is all so important. It describes one 490 year period of time that has one continuous part of 483 years, and one missing seven-year period of time that is separate. It is also remarkably accurate and exact history. During these 490 years God is going to bring an end to sin, and is going to crown the Messiah as King of Kings and Lord of Lords. It says the culmination of this plan will be in Jerusalem.

The key date that this 490-year period of time begins with, is the time when the command was given that Jerusalem could be rebuilt by the Jewish people. It is one of those times when we know its exact date. On March 14, 445 B.C., Artaxerxes, head of Persia, gave permission for Nehemiah to rebuild Jerusalem. He then said that in 483 years the Messiah would be cut off, but not for Himself. If you use the Jewish calendar of 360 day years, and go forward from that date exactly 483 years, you end up exactly at April 6, 32 A.D., and the Crucifixion of Christ. Once again we see how remarkably accurate and precise the Bible is as it deals with prophecy.

It is very important to note the event that ends the 483-year period. It says, the Messiah would be cut off, but not for Himself. We know on that day Jesus died, and thus was cut off. But Jesus did not stay dead, He rose again on the third day, and is alive today at the right hand of God the Father. So how was Jesus cut off, but not for Himself? Jesus was cut off as far as Israel is concerned. As a nation they had rejected Jesus. They had refused Him as their Messiah (Israel's promised coming King and Savior). Jesus was cut off as far as Israel was concerned. It is in the phrase, 'but not for Himself', that there is a Biblical mystery.

That phrase, 'but not for Himself', was a mystery that has now been solved. The Old Testament prophets, like Daniel, did not know that God was going to work for a while in history not through Israel, but through something totally different. That something totally different is the church, a spiritual body of believers in the Lord Jesus Christ, both Jewish and Gentile. The apostle Paul says that was a mystery, now revealed after the Cross. We will look at this distinction more clearly in a later chapter, but this verse clearly points to the church. It also points to a most important truth. God's working through the church is temporary. There will come a day when God once again will turn to Israel.

This temporary interim time between the sixty-ninth and seventieth week is the time period we are now in. This last seventieth week is the only piece yet to be accomplished before God brings the Day of the Lord to fulfillment on earth. When will that missing seventieth week happen? The week is described in Daniel as a time of Great Tribulation. We see though some things that have to be true for the week to happen. Some things that must be true, yet we are the only generation since then to see them happen.

Verse 26 predicts that Jerusalem would be destroyed. We know that happened in 70 A.D., and we know it happened by Rome. A group of rebels, what Rome would consider terrorists, has seized control of Jerusalem, had sealed its gates, and had defied Rome. Rome did not care much for Jerusalem, but it ruled the Roman Empire by fear. If Jerusalem could get away with rebellion, than it would inspire other captive people to act with the same boldness. Rome could not tolerate it, and so they moved with all their muscle to crush the rebellion. It wasn't that easy. More than a million people died of starvation as Rome cut off food and water. After months, seeing the thousands starving to death, and yet Rome still defied, when the army finally broke through the soldiers were filled with fury. They destroyed the city, burning it to the ground. Just as God had told Daniel it would happen.

But Daniel says this same empire also plays a huge part in the missing 70th week yet to happen. It says out of that same collection of people that made up the Roman Empire would arise a world leader who would make a peace treaty with Israel that would signal the beginning of the last seven-year period of time. For this to be true, for any generation to see this happen, you need two key ingredients that must be true at the same time. Two key ingredients that have never been true in any generation until ours.

The first and obvious key ingredient you need is a nation of Israel among the nations of the world. And, not only a nation of Israel, but a nation of Israel in control of Jerusalem. This coming world ruler, the Antichrist, can't sign a peace treaty for a nation that doesn't exist. He also can't sign a peace treaty with that nation unless it has sovereignty over Israel. Now we know that the only time in all the years since Daniel was told this that there was a nation of Israel was 1948. We also know that the only time the nation of Israel has had sovereignty over Jerusalem has been since 1967. Consider that! The only time in the almost two thousand years since the Messiah was cut off that there has ever been a nation of Israel in control of Jerusalem is now. No other generation could have seen the return of Christ, because this key fact has not been true before.

The other key ingredient needed is that there is a political entity among the nations that parallels the old Roman Empire. As described earlier in Daniel 7, it appears that the form of the Empire at the end, when the peace treaty is made with Israel, is not a well organized powerful empire like the Roman Empire or biblical times. Instead you see a coalition of 10 nations, and then three nations that are replaced. Out of this comes a ruler whom the world welcomes as man of peace. He will become the dominant world ruler, but he starts out as just one of the coalition of heads of state that parallels the old Roman Empire.

It is here that the story becomes very intense, for since Israel took full control of Jerusalem in 1967, almost from that time, the European nations have begun a process of uniting themselves. The Common Market has become the European Union. The plan to have open boarders for trading and a common market to compete against the USA and Japan, has now brought in a uniting of economies, and in 1999 the beginning of the Euro Dollar. Amazing. The only time this seven-year period of time could ever have been true is now. We are the only ones in all that time that has seen these two key ingredients happen.

And what do we see the leaders of the world desperately trying to do? They are trying to bring a peace treaty that will bring peace to Israel and the Middle East, exactly as Daniel said would be true as the last seven-year period of time comes to pass.

Before we see the prophecies of Israel and the European Union more clearly, make sure you don't miss this truth. Since all this is true, does your life make sense? If Jesus is soon to come and be crowned King and Lord, are you ready? I'm not writing just to give information. I'm writing so that you might be ready, and that your life might be lived in ways that make sense if the consummation of God's plan is now upon us. Make sure your life already has Jesus in the place God will put Him, as Lord and King. No other choice makes sense.

# 5 | The Unmistakable Sign

*"For I do not desire, brethren, that you should be ignorant*
*of this mystery lest you should be wise in your own opin-*
*ion, that blindness in part has happened to Israel until*
*the fullness of the Gentiles has come in. And so all Israel*
*will be saved . . ."*
Romans 11:25-26

Their names are Sharon, Arafat, Mubarak, Clinton, Bush, but they are as unmistakably biblical as the ancient Kings of Israel, Pharaohs of Egypt, and leaders of the Philistines. As we come to see in detail the evidence that we are living in biblical times we come to the heart of the matter. The heart of the matter is where God's heart lies, and God's heart lies in Jerusalem and the ancient land of Israel. Jerusalem and the events in that city have been the center of God's working in the past. It was in what would be Jerusalem that Abraham was ready to sacrifice Isaac, a symbol of the One who eighteen hundred years later would be sacrificed, the Lord Jesus Christ. It was Jerusalem that David made the Capital of Israel three thousand years ago. It is Jerusalem that Jesus said would be the key sign that would give evidence of His soon return.

In the last week of Jesus' life before the Cross the disciples drew His attention to the beauty of the temple which Herod had built for the Jewish people. Overlaid with gold, particularly the center doors, it was a spectacular sight when the setting sun shone upon it. Jesus, however, startled His disciples with the matter of fact statement that the day wasn't far off that all of the temple would be destroyed. The destruction of the temple would be so complete, Jesus said, that not one stone would be left on top of another. Something that happened exactly, as Jesus said it would, in 70 A.D.

The startled disciples asked Jesus three questions. When would that happen, and what would be the signs? When is He coming back, and what would be the signs? When is the end of the age, and what would be the signs? In the teaching sections of Matthew 24, Mark 13, and Luke 21 Jesus answers those questions. I believe the most helpful of the three to use as the basic teaching is Luke's account, for Luke organizes the teaching in historical sequence.

In Luke 21:20-24 Jesus details the signs of the destruction of Israel, and the terrible suffering associated with it. As He ends it though it is with a view of the future that brings hope and promise. He says this, in Luke 21:24, *"And they (the Jewish people) will fall by the edge of the sword and be led away captive into all nations. And Jerusalem will be trampled by Gentiles, until the times of the Gentiles are fulfilled."* It is in that statement Jesus gives us with unambiguous clarity the key sign of His return and the end of the age. The key to it all, Jesus says, is the Jewish people and the city of Jerusalem. We know that for the following nineteen hundred years Jerusalem was under Gentile domination with only a small minority of Jewish residents.

What happened in those intervening nineteen hundred years is unique in all of history. As Jesus said, the Jewish people were dispersed to the four corners of the earth. But what was unique about them is that they never lost their distinctness, and never were fully at home in the nations in which they resided. Other groups of people scattered from their homeland for nineteen centuries had long past lost their identity. Intermarrying, absorbed in the cultures they live. Yet the Jewish people remained distinct, and living within the hearts of many was a longing for

Jerusalem. In Jewish religious families as they were observant, would repeat the phrase, "Next year, Jerusalem." Generations would come and go, and yet the longing for Jerusalem would not cease. Also in many cultures they were kept distinct by prejudice, hatred, and, at times, violence and isolation in ghettos.

Yet Jesus said there would come a day when they would once again be in control of Jerusalem, and when that day happened, it would signal the end. It would signal the soon return of the Lord Jesus Christ, and the end of this age, and the coming of the Day of the Lord. It is Jerusalem that becomes the key sign that Jesus says leads to the unmistakable conclusion that we are at the end. Jesus says in Luke 21:31-32, "*So you also, when you see these things happening, know that the kingdom of God is near. Assuredly I say to you, this generation will by no means pass away till all things take place.*" Jesus' emphasis is on what we see. We can argue earthquakes, famines, the revival of Europe and its significance, but no one can deny Jerusalem. In 1967 in a war designed to drive Israel into the sea, in fact it extended its borders and for the first time since Jesus spoke those words, Jerusalem is no longer under Gentile political control, but under the control of the sovereign Jewish state of Israel.

It is the apostle Paul writing by the Holy Spirit in the book of Romans that helps us put this picture of Israel and the church together. As we have seen, God's future plan includes one more seven-year period before Jesus returns to establish the kingdom on earth of His reign for a thousand years. Yet when we see the last seven years God's focus is totally Israel. The 70th week, the Lord told Daniel is about the Jewish people and Jerusalem. It says in Daniel 9:24, "*Seventy weeks are determined for your people and for your holy city . . .*" If the focus is on the Jewish people and Jerusalem, where is the church? How is it that God turns from the church, a spiritual body, to Israel a political and spiritual body? It is here that Romans 9-11 becomes so critical and helpful.

Romans contains the summary of the great teaching of the faith. It shows us what Jesus does through the Cross and the justification that comes by faith. It shows how people are saved from the judgment for sin to come. It shows how God works in their lives to make them like Jesus, holy, as they are sanctified. It shows the promise of how they will one day be glorified with Jesus. As Paul comes to an end of that truth in Romans 8, it leaves him to answer the question, what about Israel?

Romans 9-11 is answering the question, "What about Israel and God's plans? Since they rejected Jesus does that show God is weak to save? Since they rejected Jesus is God done with them now? Since they rejected Jesus is God done with them forever?" The apostle Paul, by the enabling of the Holy Spirit, carefully answers each of these questions. It is Romans 11 that answers the last question, "Is God done with Israel forever?" The answer is absolutely not. There is coming a day in the future that God will turn His attention away from the church and back to the nation of Israel. The spiritual restoration of Israel is the important purpose God accomplishes in that last seven-year period of time.

Let me quote from this passage the key that unlocks so much for us. *"For I do not desire, brethren, that you should be ignorant of this mystery, lest you should be wise in your own opinion, that blindness in part has happened to Israel until the fullness of the Gentiles has come in. As so all Israel will be saved . . . Concerning the Gospel, they are enemies for your sake, but concerning election they are beloved for the sake of the fathers. For the gifts and calling of God are irrevocable."* Romans 11:24-29. Did you see that phrase, 'the fullness of the Gentiles'? Recognize it? It is the same phrase Jesus used in Luke 21:24 in reference to Jerusalem.

What is the apostle Paul saying? He is saying that in every generation there have been Jewish believers in the church. There never has been a time that Jewish people as a whole have been cut off from salvation. But he also says, there is coming a time when God will turn from the church in His spiritual dealings, and back to Israel. This is one of the strong evidences that supports the truth that the church will not be on earth during the last seven years, the time period of the Great Tribulation. We will discuss this later in a chapter titled, "The Day of the Disappearance." The Bible, though, clearly teaches that God has a future for the nation of Israel.

This section of the Bible also teaches why God will turn again to Israel. It says because God loves them for the 'sake of the fathers'. The fathers here are Abraham, Isaac, and Jacob. God made a promise to them about Israel that He has not yet kept. And God always keeps a promise. For it says the gifts and calling of God are irrevocable. Once God makes a promise, He will never take it back. He promised to Abraham that one day His physical descendants would possess the land of Israel, and all the nations of the world would be blessed through them.

Paul calls all this a mystery. A mystery in the Bible is something that only God knows, and we only can know it when God reveals it. A mystery could never be figured out by us, it can only be revealed by God. And this is the mystery. God is not done with Israel. We will see in the next chapter the sequence of events as God step by step brings His plans for Israel, the Jewish people, and Jerusalem to fulfillment. But let's not miss the point. We have seen in Luke 21:24 the unmistakable sign that Jesus is coming in our generation. Jerusalem is no longer under Gentile control. It is controlled by the sovereign state of Israel. We also see how the leaders of the world are desperately trying to accomplish what brings in the final seven-year period of time. The establishment of a guaranteed peace treaty with Israel and Jerusalem. You and I, my friends, are living in Biblical times. Jesus is coming soon. Ready?

# 6 | The Day of Israel

*"But you, O mountains of Israel, you shall shoot forth
your branches and yield your fruit to My people Israel, for
they are about to come."*
Ezekiel 36:8

Like a love story? So does God.
God loves the world, and God loves you, no question about that.
But God has a special love for the Jewish people, for the land of
Israel, and for Jerusalem, and there is no question about that,
either. You and I are witnessing the last great chapter of that love
story. The last chapter before the famous ending, "and they lived
happily ever after." To understand the story, and see where we
are in its fulfillment, let me take you back to a valley filled with
dry bones. It's a love story, but unlike one you have ever heard
before.

Ezekiel was a prophet of God at a time when it was not very
popular to be one. Israel had been eliminated as a nation. They
had rebelled against God too long. They were now captives in
Babylon. In fact Israel would not be a nation again until 1948,
more than twenty five-hundred years later. The people in captivity, as you can imagine, wanted good news for themselves. But
there was none. They started to complain and believe they had
no future. So God gave a vision to Ezekiel of a future for Israel in
which they would become greater than they had ever been before. In fact it would be a kingdom that would never end.

To help Ezekiel, and you and I, understand all this God spoke to him through a vision. It's a little long, but very important, so let me include it for you. It is from Ezekiel 37:1-14. *"The hand of the Lord came upon me and brought me out in the Spirit of the Lord, and set me down in the midst of the valley, and it was full of bones. Then He caused me to pass by them all around, and behold, there were very many in the open valley; and indeed they were very dry. And He said to me, "Son of man, can these bones live?" So I answered, "O Lord God, you know." Again He said to me, "Prophesy to these bones, and say to them, 'O dry bones, hear the word of the Lord! Thus, says the Lord God to these bones, "Surely I will cause breath to enter into you, and you shall live. I will put sinews on you, cover you with skin and put breath in you; and you shall live. Then you shall know that I am the Lord." " " So I prophesied as I was commanded; and as I prophesied, there was a noise, and suddenly a rattling; and the bones came together, bone to bone. Indeed, as I looked, the sinews and the flesh came upon them, and the skin covered them over, but there was no breath (Spirit) in them. Also He said to me, "Prophesy to the breath (Spirit), prophesy son of man, and say to the breath (Spirit), 'Thus says the Lord God; "Come from the four winds, O breath (Spirit), and breathe on these slain, that they may live."" So I prophesied as He commanded me, and breath (Spirit) came into them, and they lived, and stood upon their feet, an exceedingly great army. Then He said to me, "Son of man, these bones are the whole house of Israel. They indeed say, 'Our bones are dry, our hope is lost, and we ourselves are cut off!' Therefore prophesy and say to them, "Thus says the Lord God: "Behold, O My people, I will open your graves and cause you to come up from your graves, and bring you into the land of Israel. Then you shall know that I am the Lord, when I have opened your graves, O My people, and brought you up from your graves. I will put My Spirit in you, and you shall live, and I will place you in your own land. Then you shall know that I, the Lord, has spoken it and performed it," says the Lord.'"*

Did you get all that? Let's unpack and you will see exactly where we are in this vision. First we have the dry bones. A clear picture of Israel long dead as a nation. The people are living in Babylon, but they consider themselves dry bones because Israel is dead. Then the bones by the Word of God come to live, and they take on existence as a physical body. But while they are a physical body they are not a spiritual body. Here we see clearly two steps in the prophecy. First, Israel will miraculously come physically alive as a nation. Second, after some time they will become spiritually alive as a nation. Where we are right now is clearly in the in between of them coming physically alive, but not yet spiritually alive. We will see a little bit later that they come spiritually alive as a nation during the first three and a half years of the 70th week of Daniel. God will send them two miracle and sign working prophets that will tell them about Jesus as their promised Messiah and the Cross, and they will believe.

Let's go back a little earlier in Ezekiel and see how this prophecy being fulfilled has happened the last hundred years or so. God had told Israel He would scatter them among the nations because they had rejected Him. But then He tells of a day when that will change. Let me quote from Ezekiel 36:24, *"For I will take you from among the nations, gather you out of all countries, and bring you back into your own land."* Let's review a little history, looking back a little more than a hundred years.

One hundred years ago the physical land of Israel is under Turkish control. The land is a most undesirable place. It is filled with swamps. The mountains long before had been deforested. It was a place no one would want to live. But still, all over the world, when observant Jewish people gathered, it was always with the phrase, "Next year, Jerusalem." In Europe the Jewish people found themselves seemingly fully integrated into society. Scholars, physicians, businessmen, Jewish people found European society wonderful. In Russia, however, things were decidedly different.

In Russia the Jewish people had never been fully accepted. Confined to the most part in Jewish ghettos where they lived. But every once in a while a madness in society seemed to take over. The peasants in frustration and rage would take their unhappiness out on the Jewish people. They would erupt in violence and rage. Beating, plundering, burning as they assaulted the Jewish ghettos. The practice had a name, pogroms. Finally, in Russia, a generation was born that said, "Enough." We will never be at home in Russia. We will never be at home anywhere unless we have our own nation. The movement of Zionism was born. Mt. Zion is one of the five hills that make up the city of Jerusalem. It was on Mt. Zion that David established his kingdom, and thus Zionism is once again to have a Jewish nation of Israel, ruled from Mt. Zion (as has been established following 1967).

It started small. Brave and idealistic youth heading off to the land of Palestine, its name at the time. They began to arrive in the land, but found it hostile, unappealing, yet they stayed. In Europe, however, Zionism for the most part had little appeal. The Jewish people in many of the great cities of Europe found themselves fully accepted among the elite. Oh, there were prejudice and ugliness that would surface from time to time. But it would pass, and was ignored. All that changed, however, when a man named Adolf Hitler came to power in Germany, and established what was called the Third Reich. He called for a purified German race and nation that was destined to rule the world.

Few people in history have more clearly expressed the face of evil, and the reality of the Devil and his plans, than did Adolf Hitler. Satan has always known that salvation would come by the Jews. Thus Satan has had his plot over the ages to destroy the Jewish people, for he knows that God's future plans are through them. It is Satan who inspired what became known as "The Final Solution." It was Hitler's plan and purpose to destroy the Jewish people as a race. It was Hitler, who with his propaganda people, made the Jewish people sub-humans, and the source of Germany's problems. Society suddenly turned on the Jewish people. The brilliance of the German mind, and the efficiency of the German industrial world, was turned to the project of how do you kill and eliminate people in the most efficient manner. They succeeded with great efficiency to eliminate six million of them, one million of whom were children.

If we were to stop time in 1945, the idea that a Jewish state would be established among the nations was all but laughable. Never did Ezekiel's vision of the valley of dry bones seem more vividly true. Never did it seem more hopeless. There is a sculpture at the Yad Vashem, a museum to the holocaust outside Jerusalem, that so portrays this vision. It shows barbed wire, and bones caught in the wire. It is a startling portrayal of the holocaust. It seems to cry out with Ezekiel, "Can these bones live?"

But what God had decreed, neither Satan, man, nor physical/political realities stop. Out of the ashes of the dry bones of the Jewish people following World War 2, arose a miracle of history; exactly as God described, established among the nations of the world of the Jewish State of Israel. Thus, the first vision has been fulfilled. The dry bones have come to life. Israel physically exists as a nation. Yet the second part of the vision is yet to happen. They are still spiritually dead in relationship to God. But all of that is soon to change. Daniel's 70th week is about to come. Let's get an overview of that week so we can see how it will happen and we can see more clearly the steps in the process coming true all around us.

# 7 | The Jigsaw Puzzle

*"The Revelation of Jesus Christ, which God gave Him to
show His servants—things which must shortly take place.
And He sent and signified it by His angel to His servant
John, who bore witness to the word of God, and to the
testimony of Jesus Christ to all things that he saw. Blessed
is he who reads and those who hear the words of this
prophecy, and keep those things which are written in it; for
the time is near."*
Revelation 1:1-3

If you have read much on Christians and prophecy, you know that there are a lot of opinions out there, and lots of scenarios. Why is it that so many people who agree on most everything else come to such differing opinions on this subject? I think it is not because the truth is too hard and obscure to discern. I think the Bible is plain and understandable in this area as in any other. I believe also it is becoming clearer as we are living in the times of its fulfillment. The problem is prophecy is like a jigsaw puzzle. Throughout the Bible it is given in some large pieces, but also in many smaller pieces. What has happened is that people are confused as to what the picture looks like, so they keep trying to fit the pieces to match a picture, and too often it doesn't work.

I heard of a man who loved jigsaw puzzles, the more complicated and challenging the better. He had a birthday coming so a friend of his decided to give him a puzzle as a gift. His friend though had a weird sense of humor. He went to the store and purchased the two most difficult puzzles he could find. But before wrapping them he switched the tops. His friend eagerly started in on one of the puzzles, but he came to almost a nervous breakdown. Try as hard as he could, he couldn't make the pieces fit. His sheepish friend finally had to tell him what he had done. In a similar way I think there are a lot of pictures out there that people are trying to fit the pieces in and offer their scenarios. The problem is there is only one picture that is right. I want to offer you in this chapter the overall picture of the 70th week of Daniel that one last seven-year period of time. I do so humbly, but I also do so without any doubts as to what the overall picture is. I think this picture offered is the only one that does justice to the clear teaching of the Bible. Fortunately it is not unique to me, but it is one that I don't believe is always well explained.

To get at the right picture I think there are two choices that the Bible compels you to make, and the result of those choices determine where you will end up. The first choice is, how do you handle Bible teaching on end time events? Do you take it literally, understanding it is heavy in symbolic pictures, but the symbols are always interpreted? Or do you take it as story book teachings that uses exaggerations and dramatic portrayals to communicate God is in control and it all works out in the end? Is the teaching of the Bible on end time events clear and understandable, or is it deliberately made hard and obscure because it is not intended for us to know the details?

It is my conclusion that the Bible compels us to treat prophetic passages just as any other part of the rest of the Bible. As we have said in an earlier chapter, everything the Bible predicted in the past has been fulfilled in exact literal detail. It is also seen, using good study methods, that while it is heavy in symbolic language, the symbols are always interpreted for us. The symbols are all used consistently whether in Daniel in the Old Testament, or in Revelation in the New Testament. God wants

us to know, and those who come like children, without precon-
ceptions, will know.

The second key decision a person must make is whether or
not there is a distinction in God's future plan between Israel and
the church. Many people believe that God is done with Israel.
Whatever promises He has made have either been conditioned
on their obedience, fulfilled, or will be fulfilled through the church.
They see no future for Israel in God's plan. They see no significance to the current events in the Mideast and Bible prophecy.
It is a position to me that seems to so fly in the face of the evidence as to strain credibility, but still it is held by many. As we
have seen already, the 70th week has totally to do with the Jewish
people and Jerusalem. God clearly promised, as taught by the
apostle Paul in Romans 11, that He will turn from the church
back to Israel and prepare Israel to receive Jesus as Messiah,
King and Lord, on earth.

So, what's the picture like? As we see it remember, we are in
the transition period, the set up time. When this seven-year period begins it is not like it turns from day to night. It is not a
dramatic moment, it is one more step in an evolution of events
that we are seeing now. What is dramatic will be the disappearance of many, as Jesus takes His true church home just before
the final year period.

The finale the Bible portrays is a world moving toward a one
world government. It is a movement that has political and religious expression, but it is truly driven by economics. What brings
the world to oneness is a plan by the financial leaders of one
financial superpower nation. They convince the rulers of government and their merchants that the financial benefits of a one
world system benefit everybody. In fact they only benefit the
financial super power, which we will see is the USA, but the
rulers and merchants so profit from this one nation, they are
seduced in yielding to their power and interests.

As the world moves to this one world governing system, so
that financial markets are stabilized and controlled, the one sig-

nificant threat to the peace in the Mideast. As we know now, because of the importance of oil to the world economy, the world cannot know peace until it solves the problem of Israel and its Mideast neighbors. Peace in the Mideast is key to the world stability.

Those financial planners and leaders also realize the world is not going to know peace as long as there is such religious ferment. There will be no real peace as long as religions are at war. Thus there will be an effort to harmonize the religions of the world, and create some superseding spirituality that lets the major religions coexist, and becomes a platform for the eventual crowning of one man as a godlike leader. It appears that the eventual leader of this religious effort is centered in Rome, and is a representative of the existing Christian church.

During this setup time we expect to see the true coming to age of a global economy. We also expect to see a coming together of an alliance of nations that roughly parallels the old Roman Empire. The Bible pictures 10 nations that are the core. Their leaders are not particularly noteworthy. There are also three other nations that have one person who arises to lead them. These nations are not the dominant financial super power, the USA, but they do enter into what appears to be a political vacuum in the world.

During this time in the world there are other major factors at work. Some parts of the world are suffering terrible rates of death from wars, famines, diseases, natural disasters. Some parts of the world the economies are so bad, even the price of daily necessities gets beyond the purchasing power of many. There is also in some parts of the world increasing and severe persecutions of Christians.

The climatic final seven years begins with a peace treaty. Negotiated by the coalition of nations of the old Roman Empire, they secure peace for Israel and its neighbors. It is a peace so good and guaranteed that Israel relaxes its defenses. The treaty somehow internationalizes Jerusalem and allows a Jewish Temple to be built.

The person out of Europe who negotiates the peace treaty with Israel is the victim of an assassination attempt on his life. It appears to be successful, as he apparently has a fatal head wound. However, through the intervention of the spiritual leader, based in Rome, a miracle seems to happen. This person is healed. It is a hoax, but it appears to be true. The whole world is made to believe that this world leader is a special man of destiny who has come to lead the world into a new age of peace and prosperity. Everything seems wonderful. Everything good for the world seems possible.

Everything is wonderful, that is, except to two men who arrive in Jerusalem. These men have come from God to preach to Israel that Jesus is the Messiah. The world is furious. Their preaching of Jesus threatens everything. They are breaking the peace treaty and the world tries to stop them, even kill them. But they cannot. God has given them powers like Moses had when he went against the Pharaoh. They can turn water to blood red. They cause it not to rain anywhere on the earth. Whenever they are threatened, they can cause fire to come and protect them. The world cannot stop them, and they keep preaching Jesus as Messiah, Savior, and Lord. A significant number of Jewish people come to believe in Jesus. These will be the ones on earth who will welcome Jesus when He comes at the end of the seven years as conqueror and Lord.

During this time ominous things are happening in different parts of the world. The judgment of God on the nations for their rebellion is beginning. People are dying by the hundreds of thousands. A massive earthquake seems to shake the whole world. The prophets in Jerusalem keep telling the nations, it is the judgment of God. But the people refuse to repent.

At the midpoint of the treaty, the three and a half year point, a whole series of events happens that change everything dramatically. The two witnesses of Jesus in Jerusalem seem to lose their powers. They are killed. Their bodies are left in the open and televised to the world. But after three and a half days, as the television cameras are recording, a miracle happens. These two dead prophets come back to life, and everybody sees them alive. God then calls them up to heaven, and people are astounded to see it happen live.

At this time, with the two prophets gone, the world leader from Europe also makes a huge move. This man now declares to the world that he is a god, and he must be worshiped. The temple in Jerusalem is defiled, as the leader of the spiritual movement from Rome places the image of the world leader in the temple to be worshiped. To enforce this worship everybody is made to take a sign on their body that signifies their allegiance. Without this sign, perhaps a chip to be scanned by computers, no one can buy or sell.

This new world leader has a special hatred for anybody that has allegiance to Jesus. He first tries to go after the Jewish believers in Jesus who are in Israel. But God moves them to safety somewhere in the Southern Jordan area, many believe at a place called Petra. Frustrated that he can't destroy them, he then goes after anybody in the world who believes in Jesus. Many in the first three and a half year period have believed in Jesus, even with the true church gone. Perhaps somebody who has read this book. They face terrible pressure. They can't buy or sell. Then many are arrested and put into prison. Also, many are put to death.

At this time also God steps up the fierceness of judgment. Terrible things happen that are almost beyond description. Some seem like nuclear warfare. Some seem to be meteors from space striking. A third of the sunlight is lost in each day by the terrible dark smoke. Waters are polluted, all things that live in the sea are dying. Plagues strike, terrible and painful boils on the skin. People wish they could die, but they cannot.

Also, the political coalition breaks up when the true colors of the world leader, the Antichrist are seen. China moves from the East with a million man army. Russia comes from the North, Egypt, Iran, and other nations move. All of them are drawn like they are iron and Israel is the irresistible magnet. They meet in the Jezreel

Valley in Israel in an area called Armageddon, Hebrew for the hills of Meggiddo. Terrible bloodshed happens.

Finally, when it seems as if no one will survive, the Lord Jesus Christ returns. He comes with the saints of heaven. He lands on top of Mt. Olives and He comes into Jerusalem as Lord and King. The Antichrist and the false spiritual leader are thrown straight into hell. Jesus establishes a kingdom in Jerusalem and rules the nations of the world for a thousand years.

A lot to think about, isn't it? While some events seem to be a stretch to our imagination, I think what may be surprising is how easily what has been described can happen. We are so close to this coming to pass. Ready? My purpose in this book is not to detail the 70th week, the seven-year period. My purpose is to help us see all the elements that are setting it up. You are living in it. I do this so that you will understand and make a commitment to Christ that makes you ready. My purpose is to motivate the church to maximize whatever time remains for the Gospel.

So, let's see all this up close and personal. Let's see the rise of globalism, the key role of the USA, the false spiritual foundations being set, and the great hope that those who believe in Jesus can and should have.

# 8 | The Babylon Generation

*"And they said, "Come, let us build ourselves a city, and a*
*tower whose top is in the heavens; let us make a name for*
*ourselves; lest we be scattered abroad over the face of the*
*whole earth."*
Genesis 11:4

The story of the last seven-year period before the Lord Jesus Christ comes back and takes over the world, centers on three key players. The three key players, while distinct from each other, are all called Babylon. They are like three sons all from the same parents, distinct, yet sharing all of the same family characteristics. The three Babylons are each the key leaders in a sphere of worldwide influence. They are the political world, religious world, and economic world. Two of the three, the political and religious Babylon, have been easy to recognize. As we will see in a moment, they are both located in Rome. The third though, economic Babylon, has been a mystery. As we look at the evidence that I believe clearly identifies this third Babylon, I think we will see that is easy to recognize. The problem is that it has only been the last twenty years or so that its identity has become evident. A second problem that makes its identity hard to see by many is because the truth of whom it is becomes so staggering to consider it is difficult to accept.

Before we identify the three Babylons, lets go back to the beginning of Babylon and see why the Bible identifies these three as Babylons. The Bible teaches that God has already destroyed mankind in judgment once. It happened in the generation of Noah, when a worldwide flood took all human life but Noah, his three sons, and the wives of each. The last judgment came by water, the next one, the Bible says, comes by fire. After the flood God told mankind to disperse around the world, be fruitful and multiply. At that time, because we all came from the same family, there was only one language spoken in the world.

While God told everybody to disperse around the world, there was a group that rebelled. Instead of dispersing they built for themselves a city in the area today that is Iraq. The reason they didn't disperse is because they had it in their hearts to reject God. They were going to achieve a name for themselves against God. They figured if they gathered in numbers they would be stronger against God, and have a greater chance of succeeding in overthrowing Him. How foolish that thinking is. As the old saying goes, "Your arms are too short to box with God."

At this city they established they sought to build a platform to the heavens. Babel itself means "gate of God." Man in his pride would reach the heavens without God. This city was a whole structure; political, religious, and economic set against God. When God saw what they were doing, He came down and confused their languages. God has given to mankind a brilliance of mind and ability. When man comes together in that brilliance with evil hearts, then there are no limits to what evil can be done. So to protect mankind from himself, as well as to keep him from defeating the plan of God, the languages were confused, the unity was lost, and the people dispersed around the world.

Although Babel long since has ceased to exist, it has become the symbol in the Bible for the organized attempts of man to rebel against God. The Bible calls Babylon the mother of all false religions, for it is there they started after the flood. In the sixth century before Christ there did develop in the area a world power, a kingdom called Babylon. It though exceeded the plans of God and God judged it, and said Babylon would never again achieve world power status. Despite all the efforts of Hussein in Iraq to recreate a new Babylon, it will never happen. The spirit though of Babylon lives, for its inspiration is Satan himself. His working in mankind continues, and his strategy to create a new world government, like ancient Babylon, will succeed, at least for a time.

Today we see the spirit of Babylon reborn. Mankind coming together to once again organize himself against the true and the living God. The plan of Satan to have his substitute for Jesus, whom the Bible identifies as the Antichrist is moving toward fulfillment. The genius of man uniting is happening. Creations like the Internet, satellite cell phones, faxes, satellite TVs are uniting the world. Increasingly one culture, the culture of the USA, is becoming the culture of the world.

Let's identify the three Babylons. Political Babylon comes out of a coalition of nations paralleling the old Roman Empire. We have seen in Daniel 9:26-27 that out of the kingdom that destroyed Jerusalem would come a man of peace who would make a treaty with Israel. This man of peace would later show his true colors as one who is the Antichrist setting himself and his kingdom against the true and the living God. Revelation 17:9 identifies the location of the seat power as Rome. Rome is identified in the Bible as it was in the first century, as the city built on seven hills.

Religious Babylon is also centered in Rome as Revelation 17 makes clear. Her leader is identified in Revelation 13:11 as coming out of Christianity. The leader is described in that verse as having, ". . . *two horns like a lamb and spoke like a dragon.*" A horn in the Bible stands for a leader. The lamb in the Bible stands for the Lord Jesus Christ. The dragon in Revelation is identified as Satan. So the false prophet, the leader of religious Babylon, comes as a leader of Christianity. Though his outward form is as a Christian, he speaks as the Devil.

But who is commercial Babylon, described in Revelation 18? She is the dominant economic power of her day. The merchants of the world have become rich by her trade, 18:15. Her culture is the cultural influence of the world. 18:21, identifies her as known in the world for her entertainment. She is described with her merchants being the great men of the earth, 18:23. She lives in isolation from the rest of the world because she is bordered on both sides by great bodies of water. She is the great nation of the world in shipping trade, for when she is destroyed the ship captains observe her destruction from a distance, 18:17.

The one factor about commercial Babylon that she is known for around the world is the greatness of her luxurious lifestyle. She is a nation known for its luxury and conspicuous consumption. Listen to her description from Revelation 18:7, *"In the measure that she glorified herself and lived luxuriously, in the same measure give her torment and sorrow; for she says in her heart, 'I sit as a queen, and am no widow, and will not see sorrow.'"* As is evidenced in this quotation, there is something about this nation that makes it believe it is isolated from the problems of the rest of the world. There is something about her attitude that makes her feel she deserves luxury.

Taken together this evidence leads to only one conclusion. Commercial Babylon is none other than the USA. A land and people so blessed by God. A nation set apart for the best of what man and a nation could be. A land rich in natural resources, great in beauty. A land and people isolated from the troubles and wars that plagued other continents becomes the very driving, evil force that leads the world into a great alliance against God Himself. We will see in the next chapter that it is a nation that has boiled life down to one issue, the economy. It is a nation that believes the economy is the key to all things, for life consists in being able to have and enjoy the things that make for luxury. Like any queen, she sees luxury as her natural born right. It is a nation taught that to covet things is not a sin, but the driving force that makes an economy strong.

I wish with all my heart that it was not true. The USA in the earlier part of this century was the source of such good. It was the deciding factor in World War 2, as with great sacrifice and little gain it led to the defeat of the Axis powers of Germany and Japan. It was a nation noble in victory as it worked to rebuild both Japan and Europe after World War 2. It was a nation that was greatly used of God, following World War 2, in taking the Gospel to the unreached peoples of the world. But something happened from the late 60's on that tragically turned it all around. It is amazing how quickly and how far she has gone in three decades.

Are you ready for this? As we look at the USA, we also must look at ourselves. It is so hard to be in a culture and not be of the culture. Our study comes with great warnings from God, as He writes in Revelation 19:4, *"And I heard another voice from heaven saying, "Come out of her my people, lest you share in her sins, and lest you receive of her plagues."* As we look at her, we must be willing to look at ourselves to see to what extent we have bought the lies that she sells to herself and to the world. Prayerfully read on, and let God speak to you about your heart, as well as to the USA and what she has become.

# 9 | The Day of the USA

*"In the measure that she glorified herself and lived luxuriously, in the same measure give her torment for sorrow; for she says in her heart, 'I sit as queen, and am no widow, and will not see sorrow.' Therefore her plagues will come in one day—death and mourning and famine. And she will be utterly burned with fire, for strong is the Lord God who judges her."*
Revelation 18:7-8

There are several questions that have puzzled Bible scholars this century as they have sought to understand prophecy. The first is, where is the USA in prophecy? How could a nation as significant as the USA be absent from prophecy? Is she just part of the alliance of nations centered in Europe? A second question is, who is the economic Babylon of Revelation 18? Is this a nation, or an economic system? A third question is, what causes the nations of the world to cede their national sovereignty to a one world government? How do all the nation states, many so powerful, come to a common decision to become part of a new world order in which national sovereignty is all but eliminated? As we will see the answer to these questions are greatly interrelated.

The Bible describes the one world government, the political Babylon, that leads the nations in rebellion against God. It comes into being through two supporting Babylon's. One is religious,

with Revelation 17 giving its key description. The other is economic, with Revelation 18 giving its key description. The Bible,
though, makes clear that of the three it is the economic Babylon
that is the key. As Revelation 18:23 describes, *". . . For your
merchants were the great men of the earth, for by your sorcery all
the nations were deceived."* Thus, what is core to the development of the one world system organized in rebellion against God,
is a conspiracy led by merchants. The commercial Babylon of
Revelation 18. Who is this nation? It is the grievous, but compelling conclusion of this author, that commercial Babylon is
none other than the USA.

Revelation 18 is described as a city. How can we say a city is
the USA? The Bible is written as communication. It is not a political textbook, or a scientific textbook. Whenever it touches
science or politics, or any field, it speaks truth. But it speaks in
language that is common to people. Throughout the Bible and in
common communication throughout the ages, cities have been
used as references to nations. Babylon was a city, but it was also
a far reaching nation with many cities that covered enormous
territory beyond the boundaries of Babylon the city. The capital
of the nation became synonymous for the nation. Rome was an
extensive political kingdom with many key cities, but it was ruled
from Rome. In a similar way today Washington, D.C., London,
Paris, and Moscow have become synonyms for the nation. As the
Bible describes the city of Babylon, the commercial Babylon of
Revelation 18, it uses a city to refer to the nation. The image of a
city is kept because its biblical, spiritual antecedent is Babylon,
where mankind first organized himself in rebellion against God. All
of this organized rebellion against God, which has spiritual, political, and economic expressions, started in the ancient city of Babel.

Who is this Babylon of Revelation 18? Notice her description, for it describes the USA with exacting detail. It is a place
known all over the world for the luxury of her lifestyle, *". . . in the
measure she glorified herself and lived luxuriously,"* 7. It is a place
so isolated from the rest of the world, in part geographically, that

she feels the problems that strike the rest of the world will not strike her, *". . . I sit as queen, and am no widow, and will not see sorrow."*, 7. It is a place that has made the merchants of the world rich, *"All the merchants of the earth will weep and mourn over her . . . ,"* 11. It is a place whose people have the goal in life to live in luxury, *"The fruit that your soul longed for has gone from you, and all the things which are rich and splendid have gone from you, and you shall find them no more at all."*, 14. It is a place all the shipping companies of the world traded with, for as she is destroyed in one hour it is noted, *". . . Every shipmaster, all who travel by ship, sailors, and as many as trade on the seas, stood at a distance . . . 'Alas, alas, that great city, in which all who had ships on the sea became rich by her wealth!',"* 17,19. It is described as a city known by three colors, red (scarlet), white (linen), and blue (purple), *"Alas, alas, that great city that was clothed in fine linen, purple, and scarlet . . . ,"* 16. It is a city known for its entertainment industry, *" The sound of harpists, musicians, flutists, and trumpeters shall not be heard in you anymore."*, 22. It is a city known for its craftsman and industrial manufacturing, *"No craftsman of any craft shall be found in you anymore, and the sound of a millstone shall not be heard in you anymore."*, 22. It is a place whose merchants were known as the great men of the world, *"For your merchants were the great men of the earth, for by your sorcery all the nations were deceived."*

As we look at the description of this city/nation it is easily seen that no first century writer could have more perfectly described the USA than John did by the direction of the Holy Spirit in Revelation 18. No other nation fits this description. As the 21st century begins, we know that there has been one economy that has held the world economically together during the economic crisises in Asia, Russia, South America, that is the USA. No other nation meets this description. The trade deficit of the USA at the time I write this was 24 billion dollars the previous month. The buying power of the USA is literally keeping the economies of the world going. Neither Rome nor Babylon are shipping powers. Rome is inland. Babylon is something like a ten-hour train ride from the sea. We also know from a study of Revelation that the city described in Revelation 18 is neither the political nor the religious center, which are clearly identified as centered in Rome.

As I write this, I feel like a doctor who has a great friend with a terminal illness. The doctor sees the symptoms, understands the diagnosis, but he hates the conclusion. The friend has a fatal illness and he must be told, but the doctor hates the conclusion and has no pleasure in telling his friend. I love this country. It has never been a perfect country, and its history is terribly flawed as one looks at the treatment of native Indians, and African Americans over the years as examples. But she has also stood for and done much that is good. It is a nation that after World War 2 did something unprecedented in world history, rebuilt the economies of the enemies that sought to destroy it. It has also been the nation that sent a great missionary force around the world after World War 2 that laid the foundation for the accomplishment of taking the Gospel to every nation as the 20th century ends. Despite this history for the Gospel, it is evident from the last verse of Revelation 18 that this nation during the Tribulation becomes a great force for the persecution of those who stand for the Lord Jesus Christ and the Gospel. It says of her during that time period in verse 24, *"And in her was found the blood of the prophets and saints, and of all who were slain on earth."* How ironic and tragic, that a nation founded for the purpose of the Gospel is known at the end for its persecution of those who stand for it.

Yet, what I feel as I write, seems to be what is felt in heaven as well. As the commercial Babylon is identified in heaven, it seems like the news is greeted with great shock and sorrow. The angel announcing her judgment states in Revelation 2, *"Babylon the great is fallen, is fallen, and has become a dwelling place of demons, a prison for every foul spirit, and a cage for every unclean hated bird!"* Notice the surprise. It is as if the news can hardly be believed. If this was Rome or Babylon there would be no surprise in heaven at their judgment. But if it were the USA, with its history, than we could understand the surprise. Notice the phrase *"has become a dwelling place of demons . . ."* Babylon and Rome were always pagan cities, but this place didn't start out as one, but became a place of evil. The USA, founded by so many people that had fled places where a state controlled church had become corrupted. They came to the shores of the New World to establish a place where people were free to worship God, not by the dictates of a state church, but by the Word of God and individual conscience. It is not hard to imagine the horror in heaven of a nation established by those who sought to worship God in spirit and in truth, now a dwelling place for demons and all the false religions and philosophies of the world. Notice it seems to have a number of people who belong to God living in her. The people of God are directly addressed in verse 4 as it says, *"Come out of her my people, lest you share in her sins and lest you receive her plagues."*

It is this warning of verse 4 that we must take careful note. God wants His people to know this nation and her sins, so that His people do not share in her judgment. This subject is not some debate of curiosity among different opinions. We must not allow prophecy to become a subject of abstract study isolated from real life. God has not told us this for curiosity, but so that our lives might be influenced, changed, redirected, and most importantly, saved from judgment. This discussion of the USA is deadly serious for its consequences are eternal. I have deliberately not made this book a contrast and debate with other opinions regarding prophecy, for the Bible does not give its message that way. God's Word is not given to make us smart. It is given to change our lives. Thus, it is vital that we identify the nation of Revelation and her sins, for its warnings are to each of us and all of us. For God says, *"Come out of her my people, lest you share in her sins, and lest you receive of her plagues."*

We will spend a chapter on the sins of the last generation, but the ones that dominate the nation of Revelation 18 are pride and a self-indulgent lifestyle of material abundance. They are clearly described in verse 7, *"In the measure that she glorified herself and lived luxuriously . . . for she says in her heart 'I sit as queen, and am no widow, and will not see sorrow.'"* Interesting the use of queen, not king. "King" speaks of power, force, and rule; but "queen" speaks of the fruit of that which is to live safely and in luxury. This is a nation not so much concerned with rule as it is in its own security and luxury. It is a nation that sees its luxury and self-indulgent lifestyle as her right. She is the queen, and she must be served. It is a nation that has the mentality of a consumer economy that measures life by the abundance of the economy. It is a nation that everything it values has a dollar sign on it. As it says in verse 14, *"The fruit that your soul longed for has gone from you, and all the things which are rich and splendid have gone from you, and you shall find them no more."*

I wish as I write, I looked at this passage and saw only the USA. But I am afraid I look in this passage I see too much of myself reflecting back, as if looking in a mirror. Who of us can say that we are free of a queen mentality in our daily lives? Who of us can say we are not in some ways self-indulgent in our lifestyles as compared to the needs of the world, the church, and the Gospel? I believe an important part of God's making clear the sins of this nation is a warning to His people. As we spend the next two chapters looking more closely at the sins of commercial Babylon and the world as it enters the seven-year period of the Tribulation, it will be important for this truth to search out our hearts, choices, values, lifestyle.

What about you? As we began this book, it was with the question what would it be like to live in biblical times and find your life being written about in the Bible? Well the truth is you are living in biblical times, and your life is one of the lives described in the Bible. As we look at the issues that concern God with our generation, it gives each of us the chance to identify ourselves as to where we are. Ultimately all truth of God comes down to one issue, will I obey Him or will I refuse Him? God wants love, but He is God, and we love God by obeying Him. Jesus says in John 14:23-24, *"If any one loves Me, he will keep My word; and My Father will love him, and We will come to him and make Our home with him. He who does not love me does not keep My words; and the word which you hear is not Mine, but the Father who sent Me."* It is the sign of the last generation, even inside the church, that they will not obey God and submit to His truth. In 2 Thessalonians as it describes the deceived last generation, it gives the issue in 2:10, *". . . those who perish because they did not receive the love of the truth, that they may be saved."* May God help you to let this study be a searchlight into your heart. May what it reveals about you that is good be confirmed and strengthened. But what it reveals about you that is wrong may God lead you to repentance and to change. Let's see what this is all about, for this truth is about us, and where we stand before God. Let us remember, it is never too late to repent, call on God for forgiveness, and begin right where you are the radical direction of life of becoming a totally committed follower of the Lord Jesus Christ. There is time, but not much. There is really only right now, for in right now is the choice of all eternity. Make it for Christ and His kingdom.

# 10 | The Day of Globalization

*" . . . For your merchants were the great men of the earth,
for by your sorcery all the nations were deceived."*
Revelation 18:23

How does the world get to one world government, one world religious system? How do the nation states of the world get to the point of yielding their national sovereignty to a one world system? Revelation 18 says they are not led there by political or religious philosophies. They are not led by idealists who envision a world filled with peace and love. They are led by hard nosed, pragmatic businessmen, what Revelation 18 calls the 'merchants'. They are seduced by these merchants from commercial Babylon, who develop a conspiracy with the rulers and merchants of the other nations, that leads to this one world system. As we have seen the nation that leads the conspiracy is the USA.

Now all modern culture loves to laugh at conspiracy theorists. Yet the Bible clearly describes a conspiracy by the merchants of the USA. Their 'sorcery' deceived the nations. Now I do not believe these are men who have sat down and made a pact with the Devil. I don't believe they are closet Satanists who are hatching a plot to crown Satan as the true god. They are definitely used to accomplish that for Satan. But the sobering reality is that they are what America is best known for, pragmatic businessmen who are pursuing the goal of how they can best maximize profits.

These are the ones who set up the world for Satan's master plan of world dominance. These men have no love of country, no love of God. They are driven by the love of the bottom line, profits. They ask themselves, how can we maximize our profits and have a secure world economy for investments?

These are men, who in the 1950's realized that nuclear weapons had forever changed the nature of war. Before merchants had made great profits out of war. Every once in a while, wars were good for business. But world war cannot be tolerated anymore. The nuclear and biological weapons available threaten the very survivability of life on the planet. Thus, the merchants in the 1950's asked themselves, what are the causes of war? The conclusion was that there are two main sources. Ambitious nation states pursuing their own agendas at the expense of surrounding nations, was one main cause. The second was religious rivalry. Religious wars, like Jews vs. Muslims, 'Christians' vs. Muslims in Bosnia, Catholics vs. Protestants in Ireland, and Hindus vs. Muslims in India and Pakistan are not good for business. The ambitions of nation states and the rivalries of religious wars threaten the entire planet. Thus the merchants concluded something must happen to change the political and religious thinking so that there could be a stable world order to maximize profits.

Now at the risk of being seen as a conspiracy fanatic, let me share a few of the evidences of the work of the merchants in creating a one world order climate in political and religious thinking. It all comes under the concept of globalization. The concept that the world is one global village and in the village some things must change, and some things cannot be tolerated. A concept of globalization that the USA in an end of the year 1998 economic report, said that 1998 would stand out as the year the economies of the world fully became global.

A key name among the merchants that shows up again and again in this movement started in the 1950's is David Rockefeller, former Chairman of the world influential bank Chase Manhattan.

Bill Moyers on a Public Television special said of David Rockefeller, "David Rockefeller is the most conspicuous representative today of the ruling class, a multinational fraternity of men who share the global economy and manage the flow of its capital. Rockefeller was born to it, and has made the most of it. But what some critics see as a vast international conspiracy, he considers a circumstance of life and just another day's work . . . In the world of David Rockefeller, it's hard to tell where business ends and politics begins."

Rockefeller and others have been instrumental in developing some key gatherings and organizations that bring together what Revelation 18 describes as the rulers and the merchants. One is a group known as 'Bilderberg'. Let me share from a document from the Internet that they presented in 1989; "Bilderberg takes its name from the Bilderberg Hotel in Oosterbeek, Holland, where the first meeting took place in May 1954. That pioneering meeting grew out of the concern expressed by many leading citizens on both sides of the Atlantic that Western Europe and North America were not working together as closely as they should on matters of critical importance. It was felt that regular, off-the-record discussions would help create a better understanding of the complex forces and major trends affecting Western nations in the difficult postwar period." These highly secretive meetings, the most recent held in Portugal in 1999, include merchants, politicians, and media representatives. They are all off the record and participants are forbidden to share what was discussed. It is interesting to note that both George Bush (1988-1992) and Bill Clinton were invited to attend the year before each was elected President. Hillary Clinton was also a recent invitee. It is perhaps in these meetings that the concepts of the 'Global Village' are developed.

Another group formed by the same key leaders is the Trilateral Commission. Again quoting from their documents found on the Internet; "The Trilateral Commission was formed in 1973 by private citizens of Japan, Europe (European Union countries) and North America (United States and Canada) to foster closer cooperation among these principal democratic industrialized areas with shared leadership responsibilities in the wider international system. Originally established for three years, our work has been renewed for successive triennia (three year periods), most recently to be completed in 2000."

When the first triennium was launched in 1973, the most immediate purpose was to draw together—at times of considerable friction among governments—the highest level unofficial group possible to look together at common problems facing our three areas. At a deeper level, there was a sense that the United States was no longer in such a singular leadership position as it had been in earlier post-World War II years, and that a more shared form of leadership—including Europe and Japan in particular—would be needed for the international system to navigate successfully the major challenges of the coming years. These purposes continue to inform the Commission's work, " . . . The idea of a unifying Europe playing a larger role on the global stage had been a driving force in the Trilateral Commission from the beginning."

Interesting isn't it, that the key idea behind the Trilateral Commission has been developing the European Union, the very political/economic entity of a revived Roman Empire the Bible describes as the key political force of the rebellion against God in the Tribulation! Again, I don't believe these leaders are in a conspiracy in which they have sold their soul to the Devil. They are just hard nosed, pragmatic merchants seeking to create a stable world to maximize profits.

Another group formed along similar lines, with many of the same key players is the Club of Rome. Again quoting from its documents on the Internet gives its purpose in the following statement: "At the time of its foundation in April 1968 the Club identified three major needs that justified its creation: "-To adopt a global perspective in examining issues and situations with the awareness that the increasing interdependence of nations, the emergence of worldwide problems and the future needs of all people posed predicaments beyond the capacity of individual countries to solve.—To think holistically and to seek a deeper understanding of interactions within the tangle of contemporary problems—political, social, economic, technological, environmental, psychological and cultural in every sense—for which we coined the phrase "the world problemique."

In this group we see the common theme, clearly expressed, that there are 'predicaments' of worldwide problems that are 'beyond the capacity of individual countries to solve.' The views that the world is too interconnected for the nation state system to handle. Again, these are not Satanists clothed in other clothes, these are pragmatic people, financed and driven by the merchants who want a stable world order to maximize profits. These are not just my opinions. I believe they are the statements of Revelation 18 being fulfilled today.

It is also certain to these people that there cannot be a world financial order, unless there is a world religious order. Nation states not only have a world in conflict, but also religious conflicts that threaten the world. Just as some superseding order must overcome nation state rivalries, so some superseding religious order must overcome religious rivalries. While we will deal with that in a chapter by itself, it is clear these same leaders that are moving the world to a one economic order, understand for that to succeed it must have one superseding religious order.

But all of this comes back to one country whose merchants are the ones who seduce the world. We have heard a lot in recent times about evil in Washington, D.C. There is a feeling that there is a great evil in the Presidency, as characterized by scandalous sexual behavior. I agree there is great evil in Washington, and certainly the sexual misbehavior of President Clinton was part of that. But I believe most of the Christian world has missed the real evil, because it is an evil that has too much seduced us, as well as the rest of the world. It is an evil that is accepted equally by Republicans and Democrats. The evil is that all things good are measured by the economy. The evil is that life consists in how much one possesses. The evil is that there is one issue that really matters and that is a good economy.

The recent cry that has led to successful political agendas is, "It's the economy." We have not only convinced ourselves that all that matters is a good economy. We have convinced the people of the world. The nation described in Revelation 18 is the envy of the world because of its rich, self-indulgent lifestyle. All around the world today we see much of the world being American 'wanna be's'. American entertainment, clothes, style is the dominant influence of the world. I have traveled to many places in the world, and wherever you see the young, you see American 'wanna be's'. Baywatch, I am told, is the most watched television program in the world.

What is best for the USA economy is the one continuing principle of American foreign policy. India explodes a nuclear device. The USA learns Pakistan is ready to do the same. She warns Pakistan not to do it. There will be sanctions. There will be economic consequences. Pakistan goes ahead and explodes its nuclear device. The USA is ready to bring sanctions, ready that is, until it is realized that Pakistan has huge contracts with wheat farmers. Economic sanctions would hurt the wheat farmers in the USA, so just as suddenly as Pakistan explodes its device, the threatened economic sanctions are dropped. It's not good for the economy.

In the 1980's President Reagan goes to Berlin and calls on the leaders of the Soviet Union to tear the Berlin wall down. The Soviet Union is called an evil empire because its people do not have freedom. How dramatic the contrast when President Clinton goes to China late in the 1990's and challenges them to choose democracy, to give their people true political freedom, because it is good for the economy. No longer is freedom rooted in high principles, it is rooted only in the pragmatic of what is good for the economy, is good. Each year the President and Congress go through the charade of giving China most favored nation status, despite their clear and repeated violations of human rights. The rationale? It is good for the economy. We cannot punish USA business for the sake of principle, because it is not good for the economy.

Revelation 18 says that the result of all this is that only three groups of people share in the wealth, and the self-indulgent lifestyle. The citizens of the USA, who see their riches and abundant lifestyle as her right. She is the 'queen' who deserves abundance as her birthright. The other two groups are the merchants and rulers of the other nations. Not the people, only the merchants and the rulers. Revelation 18:3 says, *"For all the nations have drunk of the wine of the wrath of her fornication, the kings of the earth have committed fornication with her, and the merchants of the earth have become rich through the abundance of her luxury."* See the point? Only two groups in the rest of the world have benefitted, the kings and the merchants.

What does USA money do overseas? Do the athletic shoe manufactures in Southeast Asia prosper the people who work for the few dollars in their factories, or only the merchants and the kings? Do the workers on the best growing land on Latin America designated for cattle herds and feed to supply American fast food restaurants benefit, or only the merchants and the kings? Do the USA factories in Mexico benefit the workers, or only the merchants and the kings? Do those in China who work to manufacture clothes for export to the USA, some prison laborers, benefit, or only the merchants and the kings? I am not a social revolutionary, I'm a radical for Christ and the Gospel, but we would be blind to the Bible if we did not realize that the rich, self indulgent lifestyle and lusts of the USA are bringing great harm to the people of the world, as they are exploited for our benefits by their merchants and kings. As Revelation 18 tells us, the injustice of this is storing up for the USA the wrath of God, which will come some day soon.

In the next chapter we will see these issues as more personal. For what makes the seduction possible is that people buy the lie that life consists of the abundance of what one possesses. How many things of what you truly want today have a dollar sign on them in your mind? How much of your life is about the pursuit of personal abundance? How much of your political motivations stem from a concern of what is best for the economy? As the cartoon character Pogo said, "We have met the enemy, and it is ourselves." May God lead each of us in this most important issue. God calls those who are His to, *"Come out of her my people, lest you share in her sins, and lest you receive of her plagues."*, Revelation 18:3. Let's pray as we continue that we will be willing to let the truth of God's Word examine, convict, and change our hearts and lifestyles. God help us, for the sorcery of material abundance is so powerful.

# 11 | The Day of the Queen

*"And I heard another voice from heaven saying, 'Come out of her my people, lest you share in her sins, and lest you receive of her plagues.'"*
Revelation 18:4

W hen I was a child there was a television program called "Queen for a Day." On the show some poor woman was suddenly lavished with all the goods and attention a queen would have. It was a very maudlin show as often the woman would be overwhelmed with sobs and tears as she became "queen for a day." But what was an occasional experience for a few in the 1950's has now become the expectation of a whole generation in that same country, the USA. A queen mentality that by right of birth the person has the right to be the center of the world, indulged, and live in luxury, is now the common desire of each. A nation that has been abundantly blessed by God with riches and favor sees them not with gratitude, but as the deserved expectation. As God looks at the nation that seduces the world with its evil, it is the queen mentality that He most notes. He says in Revelation 18:7 as He pronounces the accomplishment of her judgment, *"In the measure that she glorified herself and lived luxuriously, in the same measure give her torment and sorrow, for she says in her heart, 'I sit as queen, and am no widow, and will not see sorrow.'"* A sobering, even terrifying warning, that to the same measure that she lived in luxury, give her torment and sorrow. Whatever that means there is one thing I know, I don't want to be part of that judgment! Do you? Let's see the sins of this nation so that we might take warning and set our lives to be right before God.

When the Bible describes the last generation, it talks about three loves that dominate in people's lives, values, desires, pursuits, relationships. They are listed for us in 2 Timothy 3:2,4, *"For men will be lovers of themselves, lovers of money . . . lovers of pleasure rather than lovers of God."* The love of self, the love of money, the love of pleasure, and no real love of God is the deadly combination that leads a person, society, and eventually the soul to destruction. It is interesting to note in this description that they are also people who are described as having, *". . . a form of godliness, but denying its power."*, 2 Timothy 3:5. These people see themselves as spiritual, many even Christian, yet there is no spiritual power in their lives, because they do not truly walk with God. The power of godliness is in one who dies to self, and lives to follow in self surrender to the life and leadership of the Lord Jesus Christ. Jesus warned in Matthew 7:21-23, that many in our day would say they call Jesus 'Lord,' but He will say depart from me to judgment for I never knew you. This is serious stuff, particularly for those of us who live in the culture and its influence in the USA. Let's see how these loves work out in lifestyle choices, so that we can let the Word of God examine our lives. Surely you want to know the truth, don't you? Surely you want to live to please God and be delivered from the sins and judgment of this generation, don't you? Let's look at the sins that dominate the last days, and then the sins that dominate the nation whose sorcery seduces the world for evil. Let's be ready to repent and turn from any that are found in our lives.

As judgment comes from God during the terrible seven-year period of the Tribulation, Revelation 9:20-21, notes that people did not repent of their sins. In that list of sins is given the sin of a generation under the judgment of God. As this seven-year period is just an extension of the generation, since this is that generation, we would expect to see those sins dominating today. And as we will see, we do see them dominating today. Consider the list, *"But the rest of mankind, who did not repent of the works of their hands, that they should not worship demons, and idols of gold, silver, brass, stone, and wood, which can neither see nor hear nor walk. And they did not repent of their murders or their sorceries or their sexual immorality or their thefts."*

The first characteristic noted is a generation that turns from the true worship of God to substitutes inspired by demons, and the foolishness of man. We are a people born to worship, because we were created for the worship of God. But having turned from God, we must have our substitutes. As the Eastern religions have spread to the West, they have brought their idols to worship. But so are churches filled with idols, statues, icons, substitute figures of the supposed mother of heaven, or saints that supposedly can intercede for us with God. But our search for idols to worship has lead to a culture filled with icons. The great houses of worship in the USA are now the sport arenas. Athletes presented as godlike figures with abilities beyond the rest of the mere mortals. Rock concerts with lighting and staging make the artists into godlike figures who lead the masses in a worship experience. Name brand clothes sought for their names are thought to bring an identity of worth and value to the person. The culture icons die, and people make shrines of flowers, candles to mourn as if their god or goddess who brought meaning to life has died.

The list goes on with murders. Certainly this is a generation of unprecedented death. The unleashing of death in places like Africa among the Hutus and Tutsis, the genocide of Serb against Albanian, and the responding acts of Albanian against Serb, staggers the imagination. How could people so easily kill the old, the young, the men, and women? But there is another form of murder that dominates in a generation, and practiced in many places in the world, and that is abortion. Abortion takes a life made in the image of God at its most innocent and vulnerable moment in the womb of his or her mother. The millions of lives that are dispatched with medical efficiency by those who take an oath to heal, with the first commandment of treatment, to do no harm, is raising up the wrath of God for this generation. It violates the God-given purpose of government to protect the innocent and vulnerable at a most basic level. The place where a child should be safest, the womb of the mother, becomes a place of violence and death. But this generation will not repent of its murders, instead insisting it is a right of choice. It has a concept of man, rather than God's, control over life, extending from abortion to euthanasia, mercy killing, cloning. A generation that would be shocked at cannibalization among tribes in distant places thinks little of cannibalizing its young in the name of science and medical benefits to others. If the aborted baby is to die anyway, why not use their cells, parts for others? This generation will not escape the judgment of God for its murders.

Next on the list is sorcery. When we think of sorcery, we think of wizened little men who brew their mixes and magic potions, as a Merlin in King Arthur's court. Yet the word sorcery in Greek is where we get the word pharmacy. In the first century it was used of people who were skilled in mixing drugs used by people for pleasure. They did have spiritual significance, as most things did in the first century, but what is being described in Revelation is the predominance of a drug culture. The modern day sorceries bear names like alcohol, marijuana, cocaine, speed. A people abusing substances, and the ruin it brings to personal lives, families, relationships, societies, nations. And of course the leading users of sorceries, drugs, being the USA. Whole countries lie in crisis because of the insatiable desire of the residents of the USA for illegal drugs. Columbia being perhaps the most dramatic example of the ruin to other nations that has come because of the sin of sorcery dominating in the USA.

The next sin that the world refuses to repent of is sexual immorality. The Bible speaks of sex as a beautiful and holy gift of God given to a man and woman in the covenant of marriage. But

God, in His will, forbids any and all sexual relations outside the covenant of marriage between a man and a woman. Little needs to be said about the predominance of sexual immorality in our world, and its features in American society, relations, entertainment. The generation of the 60's that set out with such noble aspirations to bring social justice to society, soon turned its attention to drugs, sex, and rock and roll. If the 70's featured the so called sexual liberation in relationships between men and women, the 90's feature the so called sexual liberation of homosexuals. The aggressive agenda to declare this an accepted, alternative lifestyle, has permeated not only the entertainment world, but the education of children as well. The Bible teaches any sexual relationship outside of marriage between a man and a woman is wrong. It also states in Romans 1:24-32 that the last stage of the disintegration of a society is when homosexual relations are accepted as right. Now, a Christian should not isolate this sin above others. A Christian is not to ever become an instrument of judgment to someone in sin. A Christian is always an instrument of love and grace. Hate crimes that are supposedly justified by the teaching of the Bible could not be more judged as wrong by the Bible. But a Christian also has the responsibility to teach what the Word of God says, and to call sinful choices what they are, sin. It would be the most unloving act of a Christian to give a person making homosexual lifestyle choices the impression that those choices are accepted by God. They are not choices accepted by God and those who persist in them will face God's certain judgment.

The last of the sins mentioned as dominating the last generation is thefts. People driven by the love self, money, and pleasure having no respect for the property of others. I wonder how many Christians think nothing of copying copyrighted material and giving it to others? How many computer programs are copied and given to others? Major copyright violations are not only features of countries around the world, they are the casual choices of many who consider themselves Christians.

So, how are you doing with the list? Remember with God there is mercy, forgiveness, and real help for those convicted of sin, who want to repent, and pursue what is right before God. If any of theses sins are part of your life, there is a God who calls you to His Son, the Lord Jesus Christ, and to the forgiveness and the power to change of the Cross. There is no sin God cannot forgive, if one is willing to repent, and comes through Jesus and the forgiveness and the power to change of the Cross. Also, remember, that the key issue with God is love expressed through obedience. You can't go on with sin, and go on with God.

As we transition from the sins of a generation in general, we come to what dominates in God's judgment on commercial Babylon, the USA. It is not drugs. It is not sex. It is pride and a self-indulgent lifestyle of luxury. It is a people with a 'queen' mentality. It is pursuit of luxury justified by its opinion of himself/herself.

As God describes the generation, He pictures them losing all their material possessions in the fiery judgment of God. The nation is destroyed in one hour in the second half of the seven-year period of the Tribulation. It likely happens by a massive nuclear attack. It says in Revelation 18:17-20, *"For in one hour such great riches came to nothing. Every shipmaster, all who travel by ship, sailors, and as many as trade on the sea, stood at a distance and cried out when they saw the smoke of her burning, saying, 'What is like this great city?' They threw dust on their heads and cried out, weeping and wailing, and saying, 'Alas, alas, that great city, in which all who had ships on the sea became rich by her wealth! For in one hour she is made desolate.' Rejoice over her, O heaven, and you holy apostles and prophets, for God has avenged you on her!"*

All material things are destroyed in this fire, God says in 18:14, indicating what their sin was, *"The fruit that your soul longed for has gone from you, and all the things rich and splendid have gone from you, and you shall find them no more at all."* It was a nation, a people, that lusted for things that were rich and splendid. As you look at the list of things it imported in 18:11-13, you soon realize that not one thing on the list was a necessity of life. Everything on the list that was imported was an example of luxury. Even the food is described as *"fine flour and wheat."* Nothing but the best is accepted. It is a nation whose luxury of lifestyle was the envy of the world. It seduced the world to want what it had.

I was in Russia in 1993 not long after it had achieved its political freedom. A university student in St. Petersburg was our translator. As we were traveling on a bus, I asked her what the political climate was like on campus. What were students doing with their new political freedom? Her response was that there was almost no political interest on campus. Everyone was only interested in getting rich and buying the things that American culture dangled before it as desirable. When they looked at America, what they wanted was not its political freedoms and ideals, what they wanted were the things 'rich and splendid'. They had been seduced by the sorcery of the USA, that life consists of the abundance of what one possesses seducing a world.

And what do we find in American Christian culture? What the Bible warns us about, a generation of those inside the church buying the same lie, that life consists of the abundance of riches. Is it any wonder that the teaching that dominates in many places in Christian television is the gospel of prosperity? The major Christian television network calls in the prosperity teachers whenever it has its fund raising. The message is always that you give to get. God wants you rich, God wants you out of debt, God wants you prosperous. But the principle is you must give to get, and always the place you give is the ministry that features the teaching. A cynical manipulation of people who can least afford to give, promising that on that evening this special speaker is going to pray and all he prays for will have their gifts multiplied back a hundred times. You give to get. The motive is greed, or perhaps just people in desperate financial need who fall for the lie. And of course those who have a 'queen' mentality, who believe things splendid and rich are their right, soak it up with eagerness. They ignore the Word of God that says the prosperity gospel is a sign of a false teacher. 1 Timothy 6:5 says of these false teachers, *". . . useless wranglings of men of corrupt minds and destitute of the truth, who suppose that godliness is a means of gain. From such withdraw yourself."* Did you see what it says? Those who teach that godliness is a means of financial gain are false teachers.

What is the truth? Does God want us all poor? Certainly not. The truth is, God wants His people at all levels of society so that they might win their peers to Christ. God also does entrust some with significant financial resources, and there is no guilt that they should have because of that. God says to those with financial resources three things. They are listed in 1 Timothy 6:17-19, *"Command those who are rich in this present age not to be haughty, not to trust in uncertain riches but in the living God, who gives us richly all things to enjoy. Let them do good, that they be rich in good deeds, ready to give, willing to share, and storing up for themselves a good foundation for the time to come, that they may lay hold of eternal life."* Simple isn't it? Don't think you're somebody because you have money. Don't look to it for your security. Enjoy the things it can afford. Use it to bless others. Be ready to share, to give, to support the spread of the Gospel. Use it to build up real secure treasure for yourself in heaven. Invest in the kingdom of God and the treasures that are to come in eternity.

To all of us the Bible says in 1 Timothy 6:6-10, be content with what you have. Godliness with contentment with what you have is the source of real gain. The lust for more, the lust for money, is a root of all kinds of evil. Don't let it take your soul. Listen to the words of Jesus from Luke 12:15, *"Take heed and beware of covetousness, for one's life does not consist in the abundance of the things he possesses."* Covetousness is the lust for more. A discontent with what one has. It drives the economy of the USA. It is the continual motivation offered to us through advertising. It will take your soul. Maybe now would be a good time, before we move on, to let God search out your heart. Let Him cleanse you from the sin of this day.

# 12 | The Day of Deception

*"Then many false prophets will rise up and deceive many."*
Matthew 24:11

$A$s a world moves to its final expression of rebellion against God, being consummated in the political Babylon roughly paralleling the old Roman Empire, we see it is built upon two foundations. The one foundation is the commercial Babylon, the USA, that seduces the world with the lie that the secret to everything is a good economy. The second foundation is a religious Babylon. It is a superseding religious unity that presents to the world leader eventually the worship of the masses. We will look at the final expression of that in the next chapter, but it is evident from Revelation that the leader of the false religion comes out of Christianity. It says in Revelation 13:11, *"Then I saw another beast coming up out of the earth, and he had two horns like a lamb and spoke like a dragon."* Horns in the Bible stand for rulers. The lamb is a reference to the Lord Jesus Christ. The dragon is identified in Revelation as Satan himself. Thus, this false leader is seen as the head of the church centered in Rome. But while he is seen as the head of the church, he in reality is the spokesman for Satan. He speaks like a dragon. Surprising, sad, terrible, isn't it? Yet that is exactly what Jesus warned about as He talked about this generation. He warned of many false prophets. He warned of many who would come in His Name and deceive. Jesus warned that the generation of His return, would be a generation marked by the dominance of deception in the church. It is one of the reasons He wanted us to be able to recognize it is the last generation.

Before one can recognize deception, one first must recognize truth. God has given the non-negotiable foundations of truth to keep one from being deceived. All of these find their expressions in the person of the Lord Jesus Christ, and the work and significance of the Cross and Resurrection. A little over a year ago my wife and I were in Israel with a tour group. The tour had stopped at a store in Bethlehem to do some shopping. Lynda wanted a cross for herself to wear, and had also been asked to purchase a cross for someone else. But when we got into the store we found that was not an easy task because there were so many choices. You could have one in olive wood, one that was silver plated, another gold plated, another covered with pearl. You could have a cross without the body of Jesus, or one with the body of Jesus still on it. You could have them in different shapes and styles. The traditional cross, or a Jerusalem cross, or a Crusader cross, were among the options. There were crosses available to fit any budget. It was not an easy decision to choose the right cross for each person who wanted one. The impression was, though, get a cross that appeals to you and your budget. The choice is yours.

As we look at the church of the last generation Jesus warned that what we found in Bethlehem in trying to choose a cross we wanted, would characterize a generation. That Christianity would be filled with many forms, shapes, options of crosses, and the temptation would be to choose the form, shape, price, style that's comfortable with you and your desires. It is very American and very much the thinking at the end of the millennium, that choice is our right. No one wants to be told. Everyone wants choice. Yet the Bible and the Lord Jesus offer us only one choice, one option. The true Cross doesn't come in different styles, shapes, prices. What is the Cross of Jesus? Let's take a moment to look at the true Cross.

Jesus gave us the foundational elements of His Cross in Mark 8:34-38, where He says: *"Whoever desires to come after Me, let him deny himself and take up his cross, and follow Me. For whoever desires to save his life will lose it, but whoever loses his life for My sake and the gospel's will save it. For what will it profit a man if he gains the whole world, and loses his own soul? Or what will a man give in exchange for his soul? For whoever is ashamed of Me and My words in this adulterous and sinful generation, of him the Son of Man also will be ashamed when He comes in the glory of His Father with the holy angels."*

What is the true Cross? It is one found only in Jesus. Jesus calls one to deny himself and follow Him. Jesus offers Himself as the exclusive revelation of the person of God. He did not consider Himself 'a' way, 'a' truth, 'a' form of life, but the Way, and the Truth, and the Life. He was not just one of the prophets, He is the One all the true prophets pointed us toward. He is not just a man. He is God in the flesh. What makes Christianity unique is that it doesn't offer a theological system, forms and rituals, beliefs and practices, it offers the person of Jesus.

The Cross of Jesus not only is exclusive to the person of Jesus, but also to the Bible as the Word of God. Jesus talks not only of Himself, but of His words. The Bible claims to be the exclusive revelation of God. The Bible gives only one of two options, believe it as the Word of God, or reject it as a fraud, for its claims allow us no middle ground.

The Cross of Jesus also calls us to surrender. To give the rule of our lives up to Jesus. To live to know Him intimately, and to share His love and truth passionately. Jesus says to follow Him will cost you everything. But you say, wait a minute Byron, you said earlier in this book it was a gift received by faith. Yes, that is true, it is a gift. But to have the gift you must give up everything. Jesus anticipated the reaction to that. For He said consider the options. What would be the profit if you gained the whole world, and lost your own soul? The Bible always emphasizes the perspective of eternity. Our lives in this world are like the morning mist that is gone by noon. You see this book is about the promise of Jesus that He is coming again. He is coming in power and authority with His holy angels. He is coming to put away the wicked in judgment, and to reward the righteous with being part of an everlasting kingdom. Are you ready for His coming? Have you come to the point of surrender of your life, and to willingly choose to take up a Cross and follow Jesus? Make your choice right now.

While the truth comes in one form, the lie of false religion comes in many forms. Where does the lie come from? Why are there so many religions, so many variations of even Christianity? There are two sources. First is us, mankind. We are a race of beings in rebellion. We have turned from the truth of God to our own inventions. Romans 1 describes this process. God has made Himself known through creation, but we don't want Him, because we want to run our own lives. Romans 1:21-25 says, *"because, although they knew God, they did not glorify Him as God, nor were thankful, but became futile in their thoughts, and their foolish hearts were darkened. Professing to be wise, they became fools, and changed the glory of the incorruptible God into an image made like corruptible man—and birds and four-footed animals and creeping things. Therefore God also gave them up to uncleanness, in the lusts of their hearts, to dishonor their bodies among themselves, who exchanged the truth of God for the lie, and worshiped and served the creature rather than the Creator, who is blessed forever. Amen."* Thus, we see that the various forms of religions came from our imagination's, thoughts.

The Bible also teaches there is a second source of the lie, and that is Satan and the demons, and the spiritual forces of darkness. When Jesus was defending Himself against the false religious teachers of His day, He clearly identified who their spiritual father was. He said in John 8:44, *"You are of your father the devil, and the desires of your father, you want to do. He was a murderer from the beginning, and does not stand in the truth, because there is no truth in him. When he speaks a lie, he speaks from his own resources, for he is a liar and the father of it.*" Thus Satan, working in eager cooperation with our foolish, darkened minds, is the sponsor, initiator, and encourager of man's rebellion against God, His truth, and His Son, the Lord Jesus Christ.

Now while the lie has many forms, throughout the history of the church, there have been some common aspects to it, that make it easy to recognize. The most obvious and continuous two lies are to change the identity of whom Jesus is; and change, add to, take away, or substitute for the Bible, the Word of God. All of the cults do this. Most like Mormons, add to, take away, who Jesus is, and substitute for the Bible. Claiming that the church and the Bible were corrupted, Joseph Smith asserted God gave him added, new revelation. Thus, the source of the Book of Mormon through revelation of golden tablets, an angel, and special glasses. Interestingly enough, the Bible seems to have anticipated this in Galatians 1:8-9, *"But even if we, or an angel from heaven, preach any other gospel to you than what we have preached to you, let him be accursed. As we have said before, so now I say again, if anyone preaches any other gospel to you than what you have received, let him be accursed."* Thus, any form of teaching that adds to or takes away from the Bible, that adds to or takes away from Jesus as revealed in the Bible, is a false religion. The word accursed is a serious one. Something that is accursed is something set aside by God for judgment.

With their added revelation, most false cults and religion offer salvation through forms of works. They give us something to do. The Bible teaches that salvation comes by faith, and faith alone. Faith means taking God at His Word, believing Him, and responding by the loving obedience and trust He calls us to give. But false teachers give us something to do, not someone to believe in and follow. The works may be obedience to the church, its teachings, traditions, rituals, rules. The works may be forms of making oneself 'worthy' through our efforts. The lie comes in many, many forms.

While the lie over the history of the church takes many forms, when it comes to the last generation it seems to have some direct expression. In 2 Timothy 3-4, and in 2 Thessalonians 2 the Bible gives its most concentrated teaching on it, and gives the definition we need to see the lie's final form. 2 Timothy 3 describes a generation obsessed with love. But it is not love of God, but the three loves of love of self, money, and pleasure. Interesting that the Bible says the last generation has a form of godliness, but denying its power (2 Timothy 3:5). Thus, it is a spiritual generation, even one that may dominate with Christianity. But it has no spiritual power. The power is in the Cross of Jesus, surrendering to Him and His call on one's life.

Because the last generation starts with the love of man, money, and pleasure, it demands of religion that those loves be satisfied. The Bible says the generation turns from the clear teaching of the Bible, to something that satisfies those desires. It says in 2 Timothy 4:3, *"For the time will come when they will not endure sound doctrine, but according to their own desires, because they have itching ears, they will heap up for themselves teachers; and they will turn their ears away from the truth, and be turned aside to fables."*

The last generation, thus, doesn't start with God, it starts with itself. The Bible says the fear of the Lord is the beginning of wisdom. But it does not start with the fear of God, it starts with the love of self, money, and pleasure. We should not be surprised to see the rise of popular teachers who offer forms of health, wealth, success. Many churches, even those who hold onto a form of the truth, start their orientation with the desires of man, rather than the truth and desire of God. Too many telling people only what they want to hear, rather than what they need to hear.

It is also a generation that takes the love of God out of all proportion to the truth, and has all but eliminated the concept of the holiness of God. Whether you start your knowledge of God with His holiness or with His love, makes a huge difference where one ends up. The Bible starts with the holiness of God. God is holy. Meaning first that He is totally separate from us, He is as theologians describe wholly "Other." We are all His creation. Holiness also refers to the truth that God is separate from all that is evil. God calls us to be holy, as He is holy. 1 Peter 1:15-17, *"but as He who called you is holy, you also be holy in all your conduct, because it is written, 'Be holy, for I am holy.' And if you call on the Father, who without partiality judges according to each one's work, conduct yourselves throughout the time of your stay here in fear.'"*

It is also true that God is love, but His love is only understood in the light of His holiness. If I start with love, God becomes some Santa Claus type figure. He is like George Burns, particularly in the movies, somewhat bemused with His erring creation. If I start with love than I lose sight of a judgment, of a wrath of God for sin, of a time of judgment, of a hell. The popular thought is God loves me no matter what I do, so I will do whatever I want. If I start with a God of love, it is easy to believe that He wants my happiness, and whatever makes me happy must be right. If riches make me happy, if health makes me happy, if ending my marriage makes me happy, if sex outside marriage makes me happy, if homosexual love makes me happy, it is easy to justify it in view of a God of 'love'.

But if I see His love through His holiness, I understand my problem is that I have been separated from God by my sin. I see the wonder of the Cross that Jesus took my judgment on the cross. I understand how much I need to repent of my sins, and run to God and His forgiveness. I understand why I need to die to myself and the sin that lives inside me, and take up a cross and follow after Jesus. Have you done that? This is not some abstract discussion of debates among religions, or even Christians, this is about the Way of Truth. Jesus said that way is narrow, and few are on it. Are you? Right now is the time to start. The Cross of Jesus does not come in the shape, material, price of yours or my choice.

The Bible always makes the responsibility personal. Yes, shame on the Devil for his deception. Yes, shame on the false teachers who face a terrifying judgment. The hottest places in hell will be reserved for those who mislead others. But ultimately the responsibility is personal. We demand the teachers who will scratch our itching ears. Tell me what I want to hear. It is our refusal to bow our knees to the rule of God that leads to our believing the lie. It clearly says to us in 2 Thessalonians 2:9-12, *"The coming of the lawless one is according to the working of Satan, with all powers, signs, and lying wonders, and with all unrighteous deception among those who perish, because they did not receive the love of the truth, that they might be saved. And for this reason God will send them strong delusion that they should believe the lie that they all may be condemned who did not believe the truth but had pleasure in unrighteousness."* There is the problem. People fall for the lie because they do not love the truth. They want truth in their own form to satisfy what they want.

We will see in the next chapter the final form of this false church as described in Revelation. But let us be first sure that we have come to the true Cross of Jesus. There are many options offered out there to you, make sure you choose the only one that is true.

# 13 | The Day of 'Unity'

*"Then I saw another beast coming up out of the earth, and he had two horns like a lamb and spoke like a dragon."*
Revelation 13:11

Truth comes in one form and the lie comes in many forms, but the world is quickly moving toward the lie in its final form. As the merchants lead a world to a new one world order, they realize it needs a spiritual foundation, as well as an economic and political one. There is a great need for a new superseding spiritual unity in the religious, spiritual world for the plan to have success. The religious wars and tensions that are in so many places at the end of this millennium need to cease if the new world order is to happen. We see all around us the efforts to lay the foundation for this unity. There is a concept of tolerance now current in the cultural leaders and media. An old tolerance gave people the right to their convictions as to truth, but to respect the right of others to disagree and believe differently. But the new tolerance will not allow one to hold a belief of exclusive truth. If I say the way I believe is true, and yours are not, than I am intolerant to you. Truth is whatever you say it is, the new tolerance says, and no one has the right to raise their claim to truth over others. In the new language people who believe that their way is the truth, find themselves described as extremists and receives the dreaded 'radical fundamentalist' label. Hate crime legislation is formed for those who declare another lifestyle wrong or 'sinful', for that is intolerant and leads to hate. All of this is part of the plan that is swiftly moving to a new superseding spiritual world order.

It is not my effort in this book to be political or to attack individuals, but to just bring the light of the knowledge of the Bible to our generation. One man who seems to be clearly in 'tune' with the new world order and needed new spirituality needed for it to succeed is Al Gore. He has used a twin approach to this new world order. One is the environment. Claiming that the environment of the planet is at risk, and that the problem is too big for any nation to solve, he argues that a new world order is needed for the sake of the survival of the planet. He advocates that the global village cannot tolerate those whose environment habits threaten the health and security of the planet. This is a strong foundation for the new world order, as it established in its theory that the problems are too big and too interconnected for any nation, or group of nations to solve.

Closely allied with this in Gore's agenda, is also the need for a new spiritual world order. He had an opportunity in 1999 to bring this twin foundation for a new world order together. It was the anniversary of the nuclear disaster at Chernobyl. While the platform was on threats to the environment, Gore used the moment to advocate a new spiritual world order. Let me quote extensively from his speech, for it so clearly expresses the philosophy that leads to the superseding world spiritual order. Notice as he speaks the call for a new, evolved spiritual world order and the heavy use of spiritual language:

> "In fact the real lesson of Chernobyl is the need for redemption . . . But we can be redeemed. The truth, as we have been taught, will set us free. And the truth taught by Chernobyl is that we are all interconnected forever. The truth is that a new time has come in which we have to make a choice . . . We have the power to learn to be human in a better way now. Of course, we've tried to

adapt to global conflicts and scarce resources technologically and materially. But the lesson of Chernobyl as our children's faces alone can teach us, is that we have the great gift of the opportunity to adapt now spiritually as well. We can evolve now, not just with our tools and technologies, but with our hearts.

And we must. For one thing, fratricidal conflicts still tear at our world. And new weapons make the potential consequences much greater. Only in our hearts will we find a new way to healing.

And what is the difference between the Bosnians and Serbs? Between Catholics and Protestants in Northern Ireland? Between Jews and Arabs in the Middle East? All, it's true, worship God in different ways. But it is the same God. And I'll wager from the depth of my convictions that from God's point of view, looking down on Chernobyl and the rest of the world, he sees one family.

In India and Pakistan, one finds some of the most ancient and deepest spiritual traditions on the planet. One finds hundreds and hundreds of millions of people who lead their entire lives in the bosom of their religious beliefs. They know in the depth of their souls that if we dedicate the human mind to overcome hatred, we can curb the evil impulse to use this new technology to destroy. They know how to use the wisdom of Islam and Hinduism to illustrate our brotherhood and sisterhood. All the great religions teach that we must act as though we are parents of one another's children, with responsibility for their well being. That truth will save us.

The challenge of Chernobyl is to recognize the circumference of our responsibility has become the earth itself . . . Humankind has never fully practiced this wisdom before. But survival has not demanded it before, and it does now. This is, as historians say, an 'open mo-

ment' a tremendous moment of choice that every nation
can seize not merely to survive, but to grow and thrive."

In this speech we see thinking not unique to Gore, but reflective
of the cultural leaders moving a world to a new world order. Key,
as Gore says, is that the world evolves spiritually. That the differences of religions are not significant, because they are about the
same God. That there is a power in human meditation as evidenced in India and Pakistan. That if we put our minds together,
we can bring in this new order. That we have a special moment,
but the need is to evolve spiritually.

As the religions or the world move to this new superseding
world order, they need a leader. The Bible identifies the leader
as coming from Christianity. He joins with the merchants and the
kings, and the leader of the revived Roman Empire to bring in
the new world order. He is identified in Revelation 13:11, *"Then
I saw another beast coming up out of the earth, and he had two
horns like a lamb and spoke like a dragon."* In 2 Thessalonians
2:3 it says there will be a great apostasy, a great falling away from
true faith that comes to the church. In Revelation 17:18 the leader
of the fallen church is identified as located in Rome.

As the apostle John sees this union of a fallen church and
the world leader that Satan has raised up he is astounded. For
Revelation ties this leader and the teaching of the false church
back to Babel, back to Babylon. Babel, the place man first
organized himself to become 'god' without the true God.
Revelation 17:4-5 gives the tie between the fallen church, the
false prophet and Babylon, *"The woman was arrayed in purple
and scarlet, and adorned with gold and precious stones and pearls,
having in her hand a golden cup full of abominations and the
filthiness of her fornication. And on her forehead a name was
written: MYSTERY, BABYLON THE GREAT, THE MOTHER OF
HARLOTS AND OF THE ABOMINATION OF THE EARTH."*

Who is this leader, the false prophet who allies with the Antichrist? It appears only one person fits the description. This

person has two horns like a lamb, yet speaks like a dragon. Horns are used in the Bible to describe a leader, a ruler. The lamb of course a representative of the Lord Jesus Christ. This one claims to be the ruler of the church, the spokesman for the Lord Jesus Christ. Yet he is really the voice of the dragon, Satan himself. It is also a head of the church located in Rome. It is hard to come to any other conclusion than that this is the Pope, leader of the Roman Catholic Church. A church, interestingly enough, that has established its identity with Rome, not Jerusalem the city of God.

Though the apostle John marveled at the identity of the false prophet, if he had lived through the time period since, he would not be surprised. If you think back to how to recognize false teaching from the last chapter, we know the elements to look for. Teaching that takes us away from the Bible, the Lord Jesus Christ, and the Cross. Let me offer in a spirit of love, but with a commitment to the truth, some characteristics of this false church that have been evident over the centuries. I take no pleasure in this, but those who are committed to God must be committed to the truth no matter where it leads one, no matter what its cost, no matter how uncomfortable its conclusions.

When Jesus was addressing the churches in Revelation, He took note of a practice that was beginning in the church. A practice that He said He hated. It is a group of people and a teaching called the 'Nicolatians.' The word nicoatian in Greek is made up of two words. One is to overcome. The other is people. Thus, the Nicolatians were those who set themselves up over people. It appears evident that this is the beginning development of a class of priests, separate from other Christians, who were to be over the other Christians. It is a practice that Jesus hates. He warned of this and addressed it directly in Matthew 23:8-11, *"But you do not be called 'Rabbi'; for One is your Teacher, the Christ, and you are all brethren. Do not call anyone on earth your father; for One is your Father, He who is in heaven. And do not be called teacher; for One is your Teacher, the Christ. But he who is greatest among you shall be your servant."*

Jesus said we are all brethren. We are to call no one "Father" for we have One Father in heaven. Yet the Roman Catholic Church, and others, in direct violation of Jesus' clear teaching has established a hierarchy of priests in the church, who are to be called 'Father' and the leader is the ultimate father, the 'Holy Father'. Also, the idea of a celibate priesthood, seems to fit into the warning of 1 Timothy 4:3 to those who find a spirituality in forbidding to marry.

We also find this church puts its teachings, traditions, and decrees over the Bible. This church has always put its teaching alongside the teaching of the Bible, and in fact over the teaching of the Bible, for the church claims that only it is the true interpreter of the Bible and what it means. The teaching of 1 John 2:20, that all believers have an anointing of the Holy Sprit and can understand and interpret Scriptures for themselves, is overridden in the teaching of the Roman Catholic Church.

We also see in the elevation of Mary a direct tie to the mystery religions of Babylon. The concept of a "Queen of Heaven" who is able to intercede for us with the "Gods" is common to many religions. The Roman Catholic Church in its gradual elevation of Mary, now has her approaching the role of co-redeemer with Christ. The Bible says in 1 Timothy 2:5 that there is One mediator between God and man, as it says, *"For there is one God and one Mediator between God and men, the Man Christ Jesus."* Not church designated saints, nor Mary, not anyone else can bring us to God, and mediate on our behalf with God, but Jesus. The substitute of a Pope as a focus on earth, and Mary as the 'Queen' in heaven directly takes away the unique, unshared role of the Lord Jesus Christ.

The elements of the Roman Catholic Church that led to the Reformation in protest against her false teachings still continue. The cry of the Reformation, "Christ Alone, The Word Alone, Faith Alone," are still the issues that divide. And these have not happened in innocence, any more than the last deception of this church, being used to create a superseding new religion will be.

The Bible indicates the final form of this will not be Christianity. It will be something new, but it will be led to it by this false church. The final form will be when the leader of the political government declares himself to be a 'god.' As Satan, the great imitator, offers his substitute for Jesus, as Messiah. Daniel 11:36-39 describes it this way; *"Then the king shall do according to his own will; he shall exalt and magnify himself above every god, shall speak blasphemy against the God of gods, and shall prosper till the wrath has become accomplished; for what has been determined shall be done. He shall regard neither the God of his fathers nor the desire of women, nor regard any god; for he shall exalt himself above them all. But in their place he shall honor a god of fortresses; and a god which his fathers did not know he shall honor with gold and silver, with precious stones and pleasant things. Thus he shall act against the strongest fortresses with a foreign god, which he shall acknowledge, and advance its glory; and he shall cause them to rule over many, and divide the land for gain."* We will see later how the false church gives this person a platform to be seen by the nations as a man of destiny, who has been set apart to lead the new world order.

Where does this leave us now? It leaves us needing the same pursuits that lead to truth. They have not changed. "Christ Alone, The Word Alone, Faith Alone." Don't let the deception take you. Let these words lead you to your own commitment to Christ. As we have said before, shame on those who bring the deception, but the deception has opportunity because people reject the truth. Don't let that be you!

# 14 | The Day of Europe

# (New Rome)

*"And those who dwell on the earth will marvel, whose
names are not written in the Book of Life from the foundation of the world, when they see the beast that was, and is
not, and yet is."*
Revelation 17:8

As we read the Bible, we see
it is the unique Book of all time. It claims to be the Word of God.
It claims to be the message of God to us, in fact everything we
need to know about God, salvation, and life to please Him. How
do we know it is true? Is faith blind? The Bible never asks us for
blind faith. It takes faith to believe, no question. But it is a faith
based on evidence and reason. It offers us not only Jesus, as
Savior and Lord, it also offers us the witness of an empty tomb.
The witness of the apostles who went from frightened men in
hiding during the Cross, to bold witnesses of a resurrected Jesus,
even in the face of death. In fact all history tells that all but the
apostle John were martyred for the witness of a resurrected Jesus
Christ as Savior and Lord. Their witness demands for us to answer, who would die for a lie? Who would die for a fraud? Perhaps
one of the apostles might have died for a lie, but each and every
one of them but John? No, I don't think so. Even John, as an

elderly man, was sent to a prison island of Rome called Patmos, for his witness that Jesus is the resurrected Savior and Lord. Yes, the Bible calls for faith, but it calls for faith based on evidence and reason.

But this God, who speaks to us through the Bible, is still speaking. One of the most convincing proofs of the truth of the Bible is fulfilled prophecy. Jesus offered fulfilled prophecy as one of the powerful evidences of Who He is, God in the flesh. To our generation, though, God is giving the most amazing demonstration of the truth of the Bible through prophecies fulfilled before our eyes. We have already seen the most powerful one, the birth of the nation of Israel (1948), and the establishing of Jerusalem as its capital (1967). This nation which has not existed since 585 years before the birth of Christ, now among the nations of the world. The promise of God that one day He would bring back the Jewish people of the Diaspora to the land of Israel has been fulfilled before our eyes. The greatest migration of Jewish people to the land of Israel having taken place in the 1990s, from North Africa, and the greatest numbers of the Republics of the former Soviet Union. What a witness God has put before us! What evidence we have to place our confidence in the Bible as the Word of God to us. It's time for you, if you haven't, to make a commitment to the Lord Jesus Christ as your Savior and Lord. God has given you every reason to believe.

The Bible also talks about another political phenomenon of our time, and that is the rebirth of the Roman Empire. While its accomplishment will not be fulfilled until the seven years of the Tribulation, we see developing daily before our eyes the foundation of this Empire. It is another powerful reason God gives to you to believe the Bible based on the evidence. We have said the final organized effort of mankind to rebel against God, will be based on three Babylon's. They are an economic Babylon, a religious Babylon, and a political Babylon. We have identified the two supporting Babylon's, economic and religious. We have seen the key is the economic one that seduces through the promise of wealth the nations to yield their national sovereignty. We have seen how the merchants conspire together to lead the world to one global economy, maximizing profits, and keeping investments secure. Nuclear and biological warfare threatening the whole planet, lead to a consensus that a one world order is the only answer.

When the Bible talks about religious and political Babylon, it uses the word 'Beast'. It is part of the symbolism of the Bible. The Bible uses language designed to communicate with power. The Bible is not some clinical, dispassionate discussion of spiritual issues. The Bible is passionate, engaged, filled with emotion. Symbols are powerful tools to communicate not only information, but with passion that excites the mind. Beast is used in that way. It creates images in our mind of evil, power, threat. It is a word that communicates in all the cultures of the world. The Bible, though, while its uses symbols, always interprets them. We are not left to imagination or speculation as to what they mean. Every symbol the Bible uses, it also interprets. God is communicating to us so that we might understand and respond with the trust, obedience, understanding and actions that He desires. God wants us to know. It is His whole purpose in writing to us.

We meet the Beast of the political Babylon most clearly in two places in the Bible, the books of Daniel and Revelation. They both clearly identify who the political Babylon is, and what it will seek to do. Revelation 17 gives us the clear identity of the political Beast that is the superseding political power of the new world order. It gives us this message in Revelation 17:8-9, ". . . *And those who dwell on the earth will marvel . . . when they see the beast that was, and is not, and yet is. Here is the mind which has wisdom: The seven heads are seven mountains on which the woman sits.*" In these verses it gives us two key truths. First, that the political Babylon is an empire which once was, then disappears for a significant period of time in history, and then reemerges. Second, it gives us its location, 'the seven mountains on which the woman sits.'

It is important to know that as John wrote the book of Revelation, he was a political prisoner of Rome. He was on a small island off the coast of modern day Turkey, called Patmos. He was there because he preached that Jesus is Lord, not Caesar. At this time Rome had made its Caesars into man-gods. Annually people had to declare Caesar as Lord. John could not do that. Thus, he was arrested and sent to this penal colony. John is writing that this Roman Empire will one day be revived as the beast, the instrument of Satan, inspiring mankind in their great rebellion against God. Thus, John, led by the Spirit of God, was careful with language. He communicates truly and clearly, but subtly.

As John identifies this coming Empire that will lead the people of the world against God, he identifies the center of its location. He writes, *"The seven heads are seven mountains on which the woman sits."* Everyone in the Roman world at that time would identify the place of seven mountains as Rome. It was a geologic feature that all would recognize. Yet he does not specifically name it as Rome. It is like much of what God has done, as a wise man of other times has said, God gives enough light for those who would believe, to believe, while also giving enough darkness for those who would not believe, to reject His truth.

Thus John predicted, by the inspiration of the Spirit of God, that there would come a day when the Roman Empire would go out of existence. Now at the time John wrote, it was at the height of its power and glory. Yet, John prophesied that it would go out of existence. Which of course, it did. He prophesied that where would be a significant period of time that it would not exist. Not just a time of weakness, or temporary disarray, but that it would totally lose its existence. But then, there would be a time when it would reemerge and, as Revelation 17:8 says, *"All who dwell on the earth will marvel . . ."* It will be amazing to the world that the Roman Empire has reappeared.

And what has most significantly marked the political world in the 1990's and the beginning of the 21st century? Has it not been the rise of Europe? The coming together of the nations of Europe in the European Union? The establishment of a common economy? The establishment of the Euro dollar, first becoming an entity in 1999? What the Bible predicted is becoming true right before our eyes. As I have said, the world will not recognize this until the seven-year period of the Tribulation begins, but it is important for us to see its development.

The chapter on globalization shows how the development of unified Europe as a world economic power was a key goal of the merchants. It is declared by the Trilateral Commission in its summary statement of what it seeks to accomplish, "The idea of a unifying Europe playing a larger role on the global stage has been a driving idea of the Trilateral Commission from the beginning." What pride they have taken in the accomplishment of the European Union and the Euro dollar.

It is also fascinating to me the recent developments related to Kosovo, and the military intervention of NATO, the North Atlantic Treaty Organization, which with the USA is made up of European nations. When President Bush (1988-1992) led the nations of the world in the new world order effort to stand against tyranny as represented by Iraq and Hussein, the United Nations was the political vehicle of choice. It was through a close working of nations through the United Nations that the nations of the world came together. It was the United Nations that was seen as the vehicle for nations to resolve their differences, and to take their stand against tyranny. Many people have seen the United Nations as the means of the new world order that the Bible describes. Yet when one comes to the Bible, Daniel and Revelation, it is not New York City that is the center of power. It is Rome. The Bible has always seen the coming order as coming out of Europe, in a revived Roman Empire.

When the leaders of the West, like Clinton, Blair, Mitterand, decided that the tyranny of the Serbs against the ethnic Albanians must be stopped, it was not to the United Nations they turned, it was to NATO. Unlike with Sarajevo, and the Serbs against Croats, in which the United Nations was the entity of choice, curiously in this instance of Kosovo NATO was the choice. Russia and China, particularly among the other nations, took strong and disapproving note of this choice. When NATO met to observe its 50th anniversary, there was an expressed vision of the role of NATO in taking stands against tyranny. Also, a key result of this action has been the increasing desire of the European Union to have their own common army. Exactly as the Bible has said, events are moving to see its fulfillment before our eyes.

As the Bible describes how events would be as the stage is set for the great Tribulation, it is just about the way things are now. At the beginning this revised Roman Empire is seen as a somewhat loose connection of nation states coming together in a political and economic unity. Daniel describes it this way in Daniel 7:24, *"The ten horns are ten kings who shall arise from this kingdom (Rome), and another shall arise after them; he shall be different from the first ones, and shall subdue three kings."* In this are described ten leaders of separate nations (horns in the Bible represent the leader), paralleling the old Roman Empire, and then another king who overcomes three kingdoms. Revelation gives this same picture in chapter 17:12-13; *"The ten horns which you saw are ten kings who have received no kingdom as yet, but they receive authority for one hour as kings with the beast. These are of one mind, and they will give their power and authority to the beast."*

One interesting speculation that comes from the Revelation description concerns the ten kings who *"have received no kingdom as yet."* How can you be a king without a kingdom? It may well be these are former Presidents and Prime Ministers who use their position of respect to offer to Europe and the nations of the world, their blessing on a man to be be knighted to lead the world to peace and prosperity. It appears they nominate this leader, and part of the deal is that they gain political power with him, although it is only short lived. Once this leader of the revived Roman Empire gains his political power he turns against those who brought him to power, because of his desire for all the glory for himself.

What creates the moment in time for all of this to come to its fulfillment, is a desire of the nations for a peace treaty with Israel. Just as we see in the world today, the Bible describes a world urgently desiring peace in the Mideast. There arises a man from Europe, seemingly not significant until this moment, who offers the solution to the problems of Israel and the surrounding nations. The Bible says in Daniel 9:27, *"Then he shall confirm a covenant with many for one week, but in the middle of the week he shall bring an end to sacrifice and offering. And on the wing of abominations shall be one who makes desolate, even until the consummation, which is determined, is poured out on the desolate."*

We will detail the biblical scenario of the Tribulation in a few chapters, but apparently this seeming man of peace out of Europe finds the solution to the Mideast problems. It creates secure borders for Israel, guaranteed by the nations of the world. It includes the freedom of Israel to rebuild a false temple. With the new, superseding religious order, brought in by religious Babylon and the prophet, this new temple is not seen as a threat, but an expression of a new order.

As we see this scenario, we understand that no other generation in time since Jesus' Ressurection could have been the last generation. No other generation has seen the nation of Israel. In fact Israel has not existed among the nations since almost 600 years before the birth of the Lord Jesus Christ. It is only in this industrialized age, with the necessary oil of the Mideast, in which peace in the Mideast is such a critical issue for the rest of the world. It is also, only now that we see Europe coming together in the somewhat loose political and economic union that the Bible describes as existing at the beginning of the Tribulation. History has seen those like Napoleon and Hitler, who have risen as tyrants who through their nation have tried to rule Europe and beyond. But the Bible never described a man who came as a tyrant driven to take his nation to world dominance. Those other leaders could not have been the ones, for the coming world leader comes as a man of peace. He comes out of a loose confederation of nations. He turns into a tyrant, in fact declaring himself to be a god to be worshiped, but that develops during the Tribulation, not before.

All of this is true because God wants you to know the truth while there is still time to decide for Jesus. He wants us to know so that the church will not fall into the deception of our times. He wants us to know, as we will see in the next chapter, so that this moment might be maximized for the taking of the Gospel to the ends of the earth. Have you made your choice for Jesus? God has spoken to this generation, not only in the historical reality of the witness of the Bible about Jesus. He has spoken to this generation through prophecies dating back 2,800 years that are coming true before our eyes. He has given us every reason to believe. Don't miss the chance to present your life to Him by faith, while there is still time.

# 15 | The Day of the Gospel

*"And this gospel of the kingdom will be preached in all
the world as a witness to all the nations, and then the end
shall come."*
Matthew 24:14

It's a fair question to ask, if God
is in control and can end this time of man's freedom to rebel, why
does He allow the world to go on? As one looks around and sees
the terrible consequences of evil and suffering. The devastations
so on the rise from war, famine, poverty, disease, political oppression, drugs, why doesn't He just end it? Well, the truth is He
will, and it will be very soon, but God is not done with His work
among us yet. God keeps this whole world going for one purpose,
and that is to take the Good News of salvation to all the nations
that by faith in His Son, the Lord Jesus Christ, by repentance
from sin and trust in His finished work for sin on the Cross. As
Jesus said, recorded in Matthew 24:14, the Gospel will be taken
to all the nations, and then the end will come. That promise is what
makes the new millennium so exciting. We are seeing this promise
fulfilled. We can expect to see soon this goal accomplished.

As the history of the end of the 20th century is written from
the perspective the Bible brings, the decade of the 90's will be
known as the most important period for the Gospel of any time
since Jesus sent His disciples into the world after the
Ressurection. Few eras have more clearly seen God's hand in

history for His purpose of taking the Gospel to the nations than what has been witnessed in this past decade. The moment of greatest significance has been the collapse of the Soviet Union. This vast empire included 330 million plus people. For at least two generations they had been officially closed to the Gospel. The empire officially declared to be atheistic. Youth indoctrinated that religion was, as communism said, "The opium of the masses." Suddenly 330 million people, officially closed to the Gospel, had the doors flung open. I'll never forget being in Moscow just before the uprising that brought Yeltsin to power, and the final strings of the control of communism were cut. I was coming out of a Metro station in the square where the dreaded KGB headquarters were. Just a block away from Red Square, the red walls and yellow buildings of the Kremlin. As the crowd parted coming out of the Metro, they went around two people who were in discussion. One had an open book and was sharing from it to another. When I passed them, I realized what was going on. The Book was the Bible, and the man was sharing the Gospel with the other man. Here in the very shadows of the KGB the Gospel was freely shared. While I was there, we received word of what had just happened in the city of St. Petersburg. In that city was a great hall built for the purpose of teaching atheism. But from that hall built for atheism not only to the crowds on the inside, but through loudspeakers to the outside, the Bible was read from cover to cover. All of this was encouraged by the Mayor. Yes, what the Bible has said has come true before our eyes. The Gospel of the Lord Jesus Christ and salvation by faith in Him will be preached to all the nations.

I have been back to parts of the former Soviet Union three times since that time in 1991. This last time I was in the Central Asian Republic our church has adopted for a special focus. It was the Orthodox Easter, and there in the largest auditorium in that city, I had the privilege to preach the Gospel openly to a standing room only crowd. I gave an open invitation for a commitment to Christ to which many responded. Also, that weekend on the network television to the nation, the Jesus video, that tells the truth of Jesus from the Gospel of Luke, and gives a prayer at the end of commitment to Christ, was shown over the network several times. The city we were in ten years ago was not even on a map. It was a closed city established for facilities that produced nuclear weapon materials. But what God has decreed, is what will happen, this Gospel will be preached to all the nations, and then the end will come.

It is also interesting to note that the collapse of the former Soviet Union has not only led to the proclamation of the Gospel to the resulting new Republics, it has also led to the biggest migration of Jewish people to the nation of Israel. Finally given freedom to leave, hundreds of thousands of Jewish people have left. They see the promise of Israel and a better life, they also know Russia's long history of antisemitism. Five hundred thousand people have immigrated to Israel in the 1990's, most of them from Eastern Europe. As God has promised, that He would bring them back to the land of Israel, so it has happened.

The Gospel's advance in the 1990's has not been limited to the former Soviet Union. China has seen an enormous response to the Gospel. Happening outside the major cities, hundreds and thousands of small churches meeting in houses have been established. Despite great persecution and government opposition, the Gospel is on the move in China. It is on the move all over the world. There has been a group established called AD 2000 that has set the goal to have a reproducing church in every people group of more than 10,000 among mankind. Their goal is to have that happen before the year 2000 ends. The exciting news that comes from this group is that the goal is close to being accomplished. Another group, The Caleb Project, has adopted that goal for people groups of less than 10,000, and they are aggressively pursuing the goal. Network sites on the Internet keep track of the groups remaining so that resources can be marshaled to fulfill the goal. This is all the work of God who has declared that this will happen before the end of this age comes.

All of this movement for the Gospel comes from the heart, will, and desire of God Himself. The Bible says He is not willing that any perish in judgment. It is God who sent His Son the Lord Jesus to die for our sins. He did it not because we were seeking Him, but because He was seeking us. He is the God who has come near through His Son, the Lord Jesus. One dramatic example of this desire of God to save is in the apostle Paul. Paul was a religious enemy of the Lord Jesus. He thought Jesus was a heretic, and those who followed Him were part of a dangerous cult. He went around having followers of Jesus arrested. He even was an applauding witness when Stephen was stoned to death in Jerusalem for teaching Jesus as Messiah, Savior, and Lord. One day though Jesus came to Paul in a blinding light. He called for Paul to repent of his sins, and to believe in Him. What a difference came upon Paul. The way of Jesus he so aggressively sought to stamp out, he now gave himself with passion to proclaim to all.

When the Lord Jesus gave Paul his life call and purpose, He shared what salvation does. Paul's special focus was to take the Gospel to the Gentile people's of the world. Jesus sent Paul to preach the Gospel. He told Paul what the Gospel would do in the lives of others. He said, as recorded in Acts 26:18, go to the Gentiles, *"to open their eyes, in order to turn them from darkness to light, and from the power of Satan to God, that they may receive forgiveness of sins and an inheritance among those who are sanctified by faith in Me."* As Paul went around the Roman Empire and preached the Good News of Jesus, it is exactly what happened in the lives of people. People who lived in darkness as to the truth of God and life, saw the light of God's truth in the person of Jesus. People slaves to sin, and the power of Satan, set free. How God loves to save, and how powerful He is to do it.

What happened in the Roman Empire almost 2000 years ago, is happening all over the world today. The Bible teaches that salvation is only found in Jesus. But how powerful Jesus is to save. I have seen that power on Irian Jaya, part of the nation of Indonesia. I was there in 1991 to teach at a seminary. The center of this island is only accessible by airplane, and thus it has been isolated from the rest of the world over the centuries. There is a book about it called, *The Land That Time Forgot*. There people lived in stone age conditions. They were cannibals, head hunters. They lived in small isolated groups in fear, darkness, demonic oppression. But to them had come the light of the Gospel of Jesus. What a thrill it was for me to look in the eyes of a dear man whose grandfather had been a cannibal living in darkness. Now here was a beautiful, gentle man whose eyes were filled with the life and love of Jesus. His eyes had been opened, God had delivered him from the power of Satan, had forgiven him his sins, had gifted him with the Holy Spirit.

I have seen in the Republics of the former Soviet Union people who had formerly lived without hope. Many in the clutches of alcohol, drowning the despair that so many lived in. Yet I have seen these people come alive. The power of alcohol broken by the power of Jesus. Their eyes filled with light and life. Their faces filled with the joy of the Lord. You can tell a true Christian by the light in their eyes, the joy on their face, the love in their ways.

I have seen that power in the USA. The man who was the custodian of a church I pastored in Colorado had been in the Colorado penal system as a three-time convict. He was known as one of the most hardened criminals in Canyon City, the maximum security facility in the State of Colorado. Yet to his heart and life had come the light, love, and power of Jesus to save and change. God changed his life. He was able to get paroled. We were glad to literally give him the keys to the church. Because God changes lives, and lives changed by Jesus are really changed. What a thrill it is to see the power of God to save. I have known that power of God to save in my own life. I have found that all of life is empty until it is filled with the life, love, and power of Jesus. I have learned that no amount of possessions, achievements, relationships can satisfy that hunger that lies in the depths of all of us. My surrender to Jesus came because of the emptiness of achievement, success, possessions. Nothing could satisfy the restlessness inside me. Life was only fun when I was chasing things, but when I got them, they were all empty. How merciful and gracious God has been in bringing me the Gospel of the Lord Jesus Christ. I love the line in a song we sometimes sing in church. It says about God and His Son, the Lord Jesus, "To those who have sought Him, He has never said 'No'." Isn't that good news? Have you come to the life, love, and power of Jesus to save? If not, this is the day, for time to decide is very short.

It has been distressing to me to see that the power of the Gospel moving in so many places in the world, is not moving in that same power in the USA. The call to take the Gospel to the nations is given to every believer, every church. Yet we see the church in so many places pursuing other agendas, other priorities. So many in what you would think would be the most evangelical of churches, have devoted their passion, time, monies, resources to political agendas. Despite the reality that the Bible says the problems of society are from the heart of man, and the only hope for change comes from the power of Jesus to save, these misguided Christians have worked with passion to change the country through political agendas. Even their political agendas, in some ways more conservative Republican, than it is representative of biblical justice and morality. At times minimizing the distinctive's of the Bible in the desire to build political coalitions among peoples from other religions, cults, and philosophies. How sad it is to see as God is bringing the consummation of His plan of the ages, to find much of the church in the USA irrelevant to the moment and the cause. In fact many nations to whom the church in the USA once sent missionaries, now are sending missionaries to her.

As the Bible closes it gives one picture of the church in the book of Revelation. It pictures the church of the Lord Jesus Christ, the bride of Christ, and the Holy Spirit with open arms going to the world, with one message, come to Jesus for life. Revelation 22:17 says it this way, *"And the Spirit and the bride say, "Come!" And let him who hears say, "Come!" And let him who thirsts come. Whoever desires, let him take the water of life freely."* What a wonderful and powerful picture.

It is my conviction that this is the key reason the Lord Jesus wants us to recognize this as the last generation. He wants us to know so that we will not fall into the sin and deception of our times. He wants us to know so that we will maximize our moment in time for the Gospel. Jesus says to us in John 9:4 as He lives in the life of His followers, *"I must work the works of Him who sent Me while it is day; the night is coming when no one can work."* Peter encourages us that we can speed up the day when Christ returns. As he tells us all the kingdoms of this world will be destroyed by fire, he asks, "What kind of people should we be?" He answers the question in 2 Peter 3:12, *"looking for and hastening the coming of the day of God, because of which the heavens will be dissolved, being on fire, and the elements will melt with fervent heat?"* Did you see the phrase, looking for and hastening? The Bible assumes that it will be the consuming desire of every Christian for the return of the Lord Jesus to bring in the everlasting kingdom. It assumes that it will be the desire of every Christian to make that day come as quickly as possible. Since God has told us He only keeps it going because He is not willing that any perish; that every Christian is to have the passion and desire to take the Gospel to their neighbors, city, nation, and the nations of the world.

If God can use this book, may it be part of His work of finishing the task. Saving those who read. Motivating those who read, and focusing their lives on the purpose God has given us to take the Gospel to the nations of the world. We are so close to the end. Yet there is a need for more prayer. More lives to come, more monies to support them. This is the "Day of the Gospel." Praise

God. May He find you believing, and working. The end is near. The morning of promise comes, and so does the night of judgment. Work. The night is coming in which no more work by the church will be done.

# 16 | The Day of the Great Disappearance

*"Because you have kept My command to persevere, I also*
*will keep you from the hour of trial which shall come upon*
*the whole world, to test those who dwell on the earth.*
*Behold I am coming quickly! Hold fast what you have*
*that no one may take your crown."*
Revelation 3:10-11

Awful, beyond description terrors are coming to this world. They are coming soon. The Bible speaks of horrifying events taking place in the seven-year period of the Tribulation. An earthquake so incredible every piece of ground shaking throughout the world. Meteors striking from space. A cloud of dust so vast, either from meteors or nuclear exchanges, that a third of the day the light of the sun is obscured, the moon and stars at night seeming blood red as one observes them through the clouds. Times so terrible people will hide in fear. People who will long to die to escape the horror of the events, but finding it elusive. As we have seen, we who are alive today are the generation that will see and experience all these events. Where will you be at this time? What will you do to escape the night of judgment coming to the whole world?

There is one event in this sequence of events that we have not covered. The Lord Jesus and the Bible promise the church that there is a moment in time coming when Jesus will come from heaven for His church. The key question is, when will this event take place? There are three main theories currently in church discussion. One is that Jesus will come back for His church shortly before this seven-year period. It is called the pre-Tribulation Rapture of the church. A second that has recently gained popularity is called the pre-wrath Rapture of the church. According to this theory the church will be here for the first three and a half years of the Tribulation, but that the really bad judgments of God happen in the second three and a half years, and that Jesus comes for His church sometime immediately before that time period. A third theory is called the post-Tribulation Rapture of the church. Just before the end of the seven years, even minutes before the end, Jesus comes for His church. Which is true? One fact that is self-evident is that all three cannot be true. One of the three, or some other, must be true. It also must be true that the Bible does not teach all three. It teaches one view. Which is it? Can you know for sure? I think you can, and I want to share what it is and why you can have confidence that this is the teaching of the Word of God.

The event itself is described for us in 1 Thessalonians 4:13-17. Comforting Christians who have loved ones who have died; the Bible encourages them that they are safe with Jesus, that their bodies only sleep. Their bodies sleep, not because death isn't real, but because Jesus one day will resurrect those bodies in a form like His, that is fit for heaven and eternity. He talks about the moment when Jesus will come back with those who have passed through death. It says in 1 Thessalonians 4:16-18, *"For the Lord Himself will descend from heaven with a shout, with the voice of an archangel, and with the trumpet of God. And the dead in Christ will rise first. Then we who are alive and remain shall be caught up together with them in the clouds to meet the*

*Lord in the air. And thus we shall always be with the Lord. There-*
*fore comfort one another with these words."*

What a wonderful moment and promise! How it reminds us
that it is vital to know that we belong to the Lord Jesus. If you
don't, now is the time to make that choice. In the sequence,
Jesus brings back with Him those who have passed through death.
Jesus does not come to earth, but awaits in the air above. Those
who have passed through death literally stand up beside those
who are alive in Christ on the earth. The word to rise means to
stand up. They stand up beside the living. Everyone is changed
in that moment into the likeness of Jesus in body. Then everyone
is caught up together to meet the Lord in the air. And here is the
best part. They will never be separated from Jesus again. The
word caught up is translated in Latin 'rapturo'. It means to be
snatched up. It usually means something or someone snatched
up from danger. Like a mother cat who snatches up her wander-
ing baby kitten by the nape of the neck. So Jesus promised He
would snatch His church up from earth. They will meet the Lord
in the air, not on earth. Will you be part of that?

When is this event? The Bible says in 1 Corinthians 15 that
it takes place in a moment, the twinkling of an eye. It happens so
quickly it will be hard to see. It is my conviction held without
any doubt, that this will happen shortly *before* the beginning of
the seven-year period of time, called the Tribulation. It is my
conviction that Jesus wants us to know of that promise, so that as
we see this time about to come, we won't live in fear, we won't
work to somehow survive, but that we will with greater passion
seek to share the Gospel, and that we will be filled with great
hope and encouragement. What does the Bible say? Let's look at
the evidence and let the Bible, the Word of God, speak to us.

We begin the discussion with the direct promise of the Lord
Jesus, Himself. In two places He directly promises His followers
that He will keep them from, out of the terrible Tribulation coming to earth. In a key verse, He says in Luke 21:35-36 referring
to the Tribulation and judgment, *"For it will come as a snare on*

*all those who dwell on the face of the whole earth. Watch therefore, and pray always that you may be counted worthy to escape all these things that will come to pass, and to stand before the Son of Man."* We see first the inescapable reality that no one who is alive on earth will escape the time of judgment. It will come on *"all those who dwell on the face of the whole earth."* It is universal, all around the world, and no one on the face of the earth will escape it. He then goes on to promise those who are His, living in faithfulness, that they will *"escape all these things."* What a hope and promise He gives. Those who are His will escape all of it. They won't be here for one part of it. They will see the warning signs that it is close. As He says in verse 31, *"So you also, when you see these things happening, know that the kingdom of God is near."* Those who are His will see the storm clouds gathering, the lightning in the distant, the rolling thunder, but before it comes to pass, Jesus will snatch them up from earth.

This same promise is repeated in the Good News of Revelation, to the representation of the faithful church serving the Lord in the last generation. Jesus promised in Revelation 3:10, *"Because you have kept My command to persevere, I also will keep you from the hour of trial which shall come upon the whole world, to test those who dwell on the earth."* Here we see the same two elements of the promise. There is an hour of tribulation, trial, coming upon the whole earth. It is something everyone alive at the time will experience. But then the promise, *"I also will keep you from the hour of trial . . ."* The word from means 'out of'. Jesus wants His to live in boldness, purity, and with a passion for advancing the Gospel to the ends of the earth. They do not need to fear the future, because *before* the hour of judgment comes, He will snatch them up to be with Him. Will you be part of this group? Are you sure? Make sure today.

Now if the church taken to heaven before the Tribulation is the direct, clear promise, we would expect the rest of the teaching on the time to reinforce that promise, and as you would expect, it does. Let me share the supporting evidence to reinforce this promise that the Lord clearly gives. One issue that causes confusion is that Jesus and the Bible, refer to two categories of saints and two comings of Jesus. When Jesus was giving His promises and describing the time period, there were two groups to whom He was referring. One is Israel, and those Gentiles who will come to faith during the Tribulation, and the other is His church. As we have already seen, the key movement of God in salvation during the Tribulation is to save the people of Israel. God sends two witnesses with miraculous powers to Jerusalem, and they preach the Gospel of Jesus. 144,000 Jewish men and others come to saving faith. There are also many Gentiles who come to faith during that time period. Thus, part of Jesus' teaching addresses them. This is their Bible and source of information and promise, as well as those who are part of the church. These are the 'saints' addressed in the Good News of Revelation. These are part of the ones addressed in Matthew 24, Luke 21, Mark 13. These, though, are not the church.

There are also two comings of Jesus promised. There is the initial one, when He comes in the air for His church. As it clearly teaches in 1 Thessalonians 4, Jesus meets the church in the air not on the earth. He comes for His bride, the church. The church meets the Lord in the air. Part of what happens with the church during that time, is the judgment of reward and loss of the church. The church also has the marriage supper of the Lamb, as described in Revelation 19, before Jesus comes back to earth. There is also the time when Jesus comes to earth to judge and rule. That coming the Bible says every eye will see. No twinkling of an eye, no waiting in the air, but in great triumph and power He comes to earth. When one studies the promises, distinction must be made as to which coming is being discussed. In Matthew 24, Luke 21, Mark 13, Jesus is talking about His coming for Israel, and to judge and rule the nations at the end of the Tribulation. I think sometimes Bible scholars forget the Bible today is not just for the church, it is also the survival guide for those who come to faith during the Tribulation. If Jesus promises His church they will escape all that is about to happen, they will escape all that is about to happen. But they are not the only last time group being addressed.

That the church is not present on earth during the Tribulation is also reinforced by who the witnesses for Christ are during the seven-year period. Jesus has told His disciples that they are the witnesses of the Gospel to Jewish people, Gentiles, to the ends of the earth. Yet when the Gospel is proclaimed in Revelation, no mention is made of the church. Revelation describes two witnesses who have Old Testament kind of prophetic power. Like Moses they can turn the waters to blood. Like Elijah they can declare no rain, and it won't rain for three and a half years. They are protected by fire that strikes those who seek to destroy them. No mention is made of the church, or other witnesses. After the two witnesses are taken up to heaven at the end of the first three and a half years, the only mention of those who declare the Gospel is by an angel. It says in Revelation 14:6, *"Then I saw another angel flying in the midst of heaven, having the everlasting gospel to preach to those who dwell on the earth—to every nation, tribe, tongue, and people."* Since Jesus promised that the church would not be on earth during this seven-year period of time, we are not surprised that the sole witness of the Gospel comes through two witnesses or an angel.

Peter, in 2 Peter 2, reinforces the promise that the church will not be on earth during the seven-year period of time by pointing back to the pattern of the way God has worked in the past. He mentions two times of judgment in the past. First was when God destroyed all of mankind with a flood, except for Noah, his wife, their three sons, and their wives. First God had Noah safely in the Ark and then the floods came. When God was going to destroy Sodom and Gomorrah He first had the angels take out Lot. It wasn't until Lot had been taken safely out of harm's way to the mountains, that the fire of judgment fell. Peter goes on to encourage the church that just as God first takes out the saints, before He brings judgment, so He will the church. He says in 2

Peter 2:9, *"then the Lord knows how to deliver the godly out of temptations and to reserve the unjust under punishment for the day of judgment."* The word temptations, is the same word used for tribulation. But we again see the truth, first God takes the saints out of the way, while keeping the sinners there for the time of judgment. The question is not where the church will be during the Tribulation. It is where you will be. Where will you be?

Other reinforcing truths are the warnings Jesus gives for His servants, His church to be faithful. He said that His coming would find many morally and spiritually 'sleeping'. The day would come upon them and catch them like one caught in a trap. Yet listen to one of the judgments from God that happens within the first three and a half years of the Tribulation. Revelation describes events in sequence. There is a scroll in seven parts. Each part contains a judgment. As the sixth seal is opened, it reveals the following judgment, as recorded in Revelation 6:12-17, *"I looked when He opened the sixth seal, and behold, there was a great earthquake; and the sun became black as sackcloth of hair and the moon became like blood. And the stars of heaven fell to the earth, as a fig tree drops its late figs when it is shaken by a mighty wind. Then the sky receded as a scroll when it is rolled up, and every mountain and island was moved out of its place. And the kings of the earth, the great men, the rich men, the commanders, the mighty men, every slave and every free man, hid themselves in the caves and in the rocks of the mountains, and said to the mountains and rocks, "Fall on us and hide us from the face of Him who sits on the throne and from the wrath of the Lamb! For the great day of wrath has come and who is able to stand?"*

What appears to happen is that God causes a massive meteor to strike the earth. It is so big and vast the impact shakes the whole earth. The resulting fire, smoke, and clouds of dust fill the air and blocks out the sunlight. As it lingers through the night, it makes the moon appear to be the color of blood. Terrible, terrifying events happening to everyone on the earth. Can you imagine a church asleep during this, not knowing that it is a time of judgment? I can't. And this happens during the first three and a half years, for it is the seventh seal that reveals the events of the last three and a half years. I am glad the church will not be here. God has promised the church that she is not destined for the wrath of God. The future for us is not to live through the judgments of God on the earth. It is to await the blessed return of the Lord Jesus for His bride. He says to His church in 1 Thessalonians 5:6-11, *"Therefore let us not sleep, as others do, but let us watch and be sober. For those who sleep, sleep at night, and those who get drunk are drunk at night. But let us who are of the day be sober, putting on the breastplate of faith and love, and as a helmet the hope of salvation. For God did not appoint us to wrath, but to obtain salvation through our Lord Jesus Christ, who died for us, that whether we wake or sleep, we should live together with Him. Therefore comfort each other and edify one another, just as you also are doing."* What good news those who are in Christ have as they face the future. God did not intend us for wrath, for His wrath against our sins has been satisfied as we have taken hold of Jesus and His work on the Cross. We focus as we see this Day soon coming, on keeping our lives ready for Jesus, and seeking to maximize this moment for the Gospel.

As to the timing of this event, there is a lot of evidence that the day will come during the Jewish Feast of Trumpets, or Rosh Hashana. The feasts of Israel are all being fulfilled in Jesus. He died on Passover, as the Passover Lamb, as the unleavened bread offered for sin. Unleavened bread symbolizing that the sacrifice, Jesus had no sin. He sent the Holy Spirit on Pentecost (Feast of Weeks), the next feast fifty days after the Passover. The Feast of the Trumpets was one of great celebration. It was celebrated on the first sign of the new moon in the seventh month. It is followed ten days later by the Day of Atonement.

What makes the Feast of Trumpets so interesting is that it corresponds to the promise of the Rapture of the church in 1 Corinthians 15. It gives this description in 1 Corinthians 15:51-52, *"Behold, I tell you a mystery: We shall not all sleep, but we shall all be changed—in a moment, in the twinkling of an eye, at the last trumpet. For the trumpet will sound, and the dead will be raised incorruptible, and we shall be changed."* During the Feast of Trumpets, the trumpets were blown 100 times. At the end of each of the two days the trumpet would give one last, long blast. It is most likely then that Jesus will come for the church. The next event ten days later is the Day of Atonement. It is then that God will turn to Israel, whose sins have been atoned for, and bring the message of salvation.

There are some who consider the last trumpet of 1 Corinthians to be the seventh trumpet of Revelation. The seventh trumpet sounds proclaiming the last judgments that come in the second three and a half years. Thus, some say, that is the last trumpet, and the church is on earth for the first three and a half years. Yet when you read Revelation 11, we see there is not a consistency with this point of view. The trumpet is not announcing the Rapture of the church. It is announcing the last terrible judgments. It is not called the last trumpet, in fact a trumpet is not even mentioned. It says in Revelation 11:15, *"Then the seventh angel sounded . . ."*

But some would say, the Bible teaches no one knows the day or the hour of Jesus' return. Well, a two-day feast with a hundred times the trumpet is blown, could easily happen without anyone knowing which day or hour. In fact though, the ones that were not to know the day or the hour were the first century disciples. They were looking for when Jesus would come back, and Jesus told them it is not for that generation to know that. They were to focus on taking the Gospel to the ends of the earth. He said to them in Acts 1:7-8, *"It is not for you to know times or seasons which the Father has put in His own authority. But you shall receive power when the Holy Spirit has come upon you; and you shall be witnesses to Me in Jerusalem, and in all Judea and Samaria, and to the end of the earth."* Thus they were not to be focused on when Christ comes back, but taking the Gospel to the nations. Yet Jesus says to the last generation of the church in

Luke 21:31, *"So you also, when you see these things happening, know that the kingdom of God is near."*

There are more points that can be made to reinforce this promise of Jesus that the church will escape all that is about to happen, but the promise is so clear. The question is not where the church will be during the Tribulation. They will be safely home with Jesus. The question is, where you will be. Today, right now is the time to be sure. May God help you to make the choice for Jesus that will change your life today, tomorrow and forever.

# 17 | A Day of Calamity

*"But when you hear of wars and rumors of wars, do not be*
*troubled; for such things must happen, but the end is not*
*yet. For nation will rise against nation, and kingdom*
*against kingdom. And there will be famines and troubles.*
*These are the beginnings of sorrows."*
Mark 13:8-9

If there is one feature that has
marked the end of the 20th century and the start of the 21st, it is
the staggering numbers and amounts of calamities that have become a regular feature of life. Catastrophic earthquakes, drought
and famine, hurricanes/typhoons, AIDS epidemics, wars and
"ethnic cleansing" all part of the routine of news. Add to these
nuclear disasters like Chernobyl, oil spills, water contaminations
and there is a sense that something very unusual is happening.
We collect our fears in concepts like global warming. We try to
put these things into categories that bring explanations, yet within
we wonder what is going on. We call it the effects of El Nino, or
La Nina, routine variations in climate, yet why does it seem so
catastrophic now? We hear scientists warning us with fears of
global warming, and that we are changing the planet to the point
of putting life as we know it now at risk. What is going on?

As Jesus described the time period between His first and
Second Coming, He described times that would see continual
calamities. Wars, famines, earthquakes, diseases—all would hap-

pen throughout the time period. Yet as Jesus described them He used an interesting phrase. He called these, "the beginning of sorrows." The word for sorrow describes a woman in labor. A woman experiences throughout her pregnancy the "pangs" of her body readying itself to deliver the baby.

The closer she comes to labor the numbers of the pangs increase, and so does their intensity. It is this picture that Jesus uses to describe the calamities of the world. He is telling us that the closer to His Second Coming we come the more frequent and intense will be the catastrophic events. Thus what we have experienced as the 20th century ends and the 21st begins is another dramatic evidence that we live in the generation that will see Jesus return with reward for His followers, and judgment for the world. The fulfillment of the signs are unmistakable. Are you ready? Does your life make sense in light of the promise and warning of Jesus' soon return?

What is interesting about these calamities increasing, as the world is described as a woman in the intensity of the pangs of giving birth, is how the judgments of Revelation are just these events taken to their ultimate degrees. One of the most famous of the judgments of Revelation is the description of the Four Horsemen of the Apocalypse from Revelation 6. As these horsemen ride they bring to earth only the intensification of the birth pangs. The first horseman rides in a spirit of political conquest. He brings political domination over others. The second horseman brings war. A time of great violence, great killings of people by one another. The third horseman brings food crisis, famines, inflation, and the terrible consequences of malnutrition and starvation. The fourth horseman brings death through war, famine, disease, and wild animals turning on mankind. As can easily be recognized, all of these events are just the ultimate intensification of the birth pangs. It is a difference of calamities only in degree, not in kind.

As the Bible portrays the last generation, and the terrible events of the judgments of God in the seven-year period of the

Great Tribulation, it is not a time period of dramatic change. It is not a world that is one way one day, and another the next. It is a gradual intensification that the seven years brings to the maximum. The clear evidence from Bible prophecy and the news of our day is that the four horsemen have already begun their terrifying rides. What we see before us is a world in the throes of birth pangs, warning of coming judgment, and the promise of the kingdom of righteousness which Jesus will bring to earth with the saints. Truly, the morning comes and, also, the night.

What are the evidences of the increase of calamities? Let's give just a few examples of the many which could be given. Few continents display the catastrophes of our day in more graphic detail and staggering numbers than Africa. It seems that there the four horsemen have been given their freest ride. We staggered in the 1990's with the incredible deaths that are still occurring from the conflict among the Hutus and Tutsis. The numbers killed are now into the millions. When the slaughters found their way into the international spotlight in 1994, there were an incredible 500,000 slain in months. The savagery and butchery almost beyond imagination. Yet what was to the extreme in these conflicts has happened in many other places in the world. The world is now discovering the results of the 'ethnic cleansing' in the conflicts in the Balkans, in places like Kosovo. Asia has seen its atrocities in equally overwhelming numbers in the killing fields of Cambodia and Laos, in the eruption of violence and killing among Christians and Muslims in Indonesia. Russia has seen its own savagery in the conflict in Chechnya. The horsemen of conquest, war, death ride freely as the 21$^{st}$ century begins.

We also see the horseman of death riding freely. Written clearly as a banner under which he rides is AIDS. This ravaging epidemic still on the rise, and spreading rapidly. Again it is the continent of Africa that the horseman rides with his most deadly intensity. In 1998 there were approximately two million deaths from AIDS. It is believed that there are now 34 million people living in sub-Sahara Africa who are infected with AIDS. One estimate recently given is that 25 percent (25%) of people currently living in Africa will die from AIDS by the year 2010. It is a statistic almost beyond comprehension. Yet the Bible says in Revelation 6:8, of the consequences of the horseman of death riding, "... *And power was given to them over a fourth of the earth, to kill with sword, with hunger, with death, and by the beasts of the earth.*" What is true in Africa to the extreme is also increasingly true in India, and throughout Southeast Asia.

Another evidence of this horseman of death riding is in hunger, starvation, and famine. Every 3.6 seconds someone dies of hunger in our world. Twenty-four thousand people die every day from hunger, about three fourths of them are children. In many of these cases we see that deaths from hunger are the results of the horsemen of war and conquest riding. In places like Sudan, Ethiopia, and Eritrea it is obvious that death by starvation has been either directly a result of policy, or an indirect result of war. Both hunger and malnutrition are a reality around the world. It is estimated that 800 million people suffer currently from hunger and malnutrition. One estimate in North Korea is that 10 percent (10%) of its population died of famine in a two year period.

Added to these evidences of the increase of the calamities of our time, are the devastating earthquakes, hurricanes, typhoons, floods, volcanoes that have become the routine of our times. It is true that some of the numbers are just the result of the population explosion of our time. The result of so many people in our world living along the vulnerable coastlines of the oceans. The result of large cities being built in earthquake zones. Yet, whatever the cause, they are the evidence of the increasing catastrophic nature of our times.

One issue that many believe lies behind the extremes of weather that we are experiencing is global warming. There is the fear that by our industrializing of the planet, the great use of fossil fuels, the breakdown in the ozone layer, we are fundamentally changing and damaging the earth. It seems that the evidence of global warming is now beyond debate. As the 20ᵗʰ century ends and the 21ˢᵗ century begins we see each succeeding year warmer than the year before. Each year setting the record for the warmest year since records are kept. May 2000 was the hottest month ever recorded. This global warming causes increasing extremes in weather. It is changing rain and weather patterns. It is producing droughts in areas that have not seen them before. It is producing a big question mark over the future, and a gnawing anxiety that the future may no longer be our friend.

When these devastating calamities are viewed alone they give the clear sense that the times are changing, and the future is uncertain. When they are taken in concert with the other fulfillments of Biblical prophecies in our generation, they give the clear message that this is the final generation. They give clear evidence that the morning comes, and also the night. Israel is the clearest and most dramatic evidence of our times. No one can argue that we are the only generation since 585 B.C. to have seen a sovereign nation of Israel in existence, and one that rules Jerusalem. But we also see the astounding corresponding fulfillment of all the events that Jesus and the Bible said would be true of the generation of His return.

We need to see that these signs are the warning of God that judgment is coming. They are evidences of His mercy. If God brought judgment with no warning, it would be just. But God is also full of mercy. He wants no one to perish in judgment. He allows the disasters, calamities, catastrophes, so we will recognize our unusual times and look for answers. The Bible and its fulfilled prophecies is one of the most convincing evidences that it is the voice of God to us. God respects our mind, and thus gives us the evidence so that we can know His Word to us, the Bible. No religious book has dared to stake its credibility on its predictions of the future, as the Bible has. Now we live in the midst of events that are happening exactly as the Bible predicted them from thirty-five hundred to two thousand years ago.

God has done that because He loves you. He wants you to know the times, and to be sure your life rests by faith in the Lord Jesus Christ. He wants you to know the time for decision is about over, for the morning comes and also the night. Even the local weather report shouts out the news that Jesus is coming. Time is short. Be ready. Are you?

# 18 | The Day Like Noah's

*"But as the days of Noah were, so also will the coming of the Son of Man be."*
Matthew 24:37

As we come to the conclusion of the description of the generation alive at the Second Coming of the Lord Jesus Christ, we see the dramatic and tragic parallels between this generation and the other generation God destroyed in judgment, Noah's. Jesus said that as it was in the days of Noah so it will be when He comes back. As Jesus draws the comparison to that other fateful generation, they are similar in two ways. One likeness is in the total moral breakdown of society around the world. The world at both times was corrupt and full of violence. The other similarity is that the generation of Noah lived with no expectation of the coming judgment of God. In fact they laughed at Noah for 100 years as he warned them of coming judgment. When judgment came it found them unprepared and oblivious to the reality that in an hour they would perish and enter eternity damned forever.

What was the generation of Noah like in its moral condition? Genesis gives us the key descriptions. In Genesis 6:5 it says of them, *"Then the Lord saw that the wickedness of man was great in the earth, and that every intent of the thoughts of his heart was only evil continually."* *Genesis 6:11-13* describes the violence and destructiveness that inevitably comes from the loss of moral restraint, *"The earth also was corrupt before God, and the earth was filled with violence. So God looked upon the earth and indeed it was corrupt; for all the flesh had corrupted their ways on the earth. And God said to Noah, "The end of all flesh has come before Me, for the earth is filled with violence through them; and behold, I will destroy them with the earth."*"

As the Bible describes the generation alive at the coming of Jesus, it describes a world like Noah's. A world without moral restraint, and the resulting violence and destructiveness. Before we see the multiple evidences of that in our world, let's look at a description of this generation from 2 Timothy 3:1-6. *"But know this, that in the last days perilous times will come: For men will be lovers of themselves, lovers of money, boasters, proud, blasphemers, disobedient to parents, unthankful, unholy, unloving, unforgiving, slanderers, without self-control, brutal, despisers of good, traitors, headstrong, haughty, lovers of pleasure rather than lovers of God, having a form of godliness but denying its power. And from such people turn away!"*

The Bible gives four dominating characteristics of this generation. It is the fourth that is the most curious. He describes people whose lives are compelled by three loves, desires, lusts. The love of themselves, the love of money, and the love of pleasure. But it is the fourth characteristic that is most revealing. They are a people who want to maintain an illusion of spirituality. It says they have a form of godliness but deny its power. They dress themselves in spiritual clothes, but there is no power of God in their lives. The power of godliness is in obedience, the Cross, that dies to self, so that it might live for the glory of God through His Son the Lord Jesus Christ. How surprised they will be to learn that though they have called themselves Christians, in reality they are empty of His salvation and life. Does your spirituality have the power of godliness? Does your life evidence the surrendered heart, that hungers and thirsts to be right with God? How eternally important the answer to these questions are.

As we look at our generation, what do we see? Do we see lives compelled by the love of self, money, pleasure? Do we see the resulting violence and destructiveness in society that results when moral restraint is lost? Do we see that every intent of the heart turned to wickedness? Do we see the breakdown of family, as Paul reveals by the Spirit of God? The reality is that it is hard at times to see anything else.

Where should we start to describe the loss of moral restraint of this generation? Do we start with the Internet? What a tool the Internet is to connect instantly people all around the world. To have an almost endless source of knowledge. To have the increasing streaming ability to bring voice, sight, sound from anywhere in the world. Yet we see by far the greatest use of this tool of the Internet is to indulge the darkness within. Pornography dominates in almost any form imagined, and some all but unimagined until this day. It is said that the only successful, profit making business on the Internet is pornography. Hundreds, thousands of men enslaved to the hard core pornography, that is like a quicksand without a bottom in which they become stuck and only sink deeper.

Should we move from the Internet to the increasing development of digital cable systems to understand the loss of moral restraint? These fiber optic cables able to offer seemingly endless numbers of channels. And what is it we see increasing on these systems? Pay-TV pornography. Such mainline, establishment companies like AT&T embracing pornographic pay-TV as the featured money maker. These cable systems asking producers for pornography, the more graphic the better. Cable systems, satellite TV that find the one thing customers want is 'adult entertainment', the raunchier the better.

Where else do we go to see the loss of moral restraint and the resulting violence? Do we go to the place that ought to be the safest place in the world, the womb of a mother? No more clearly is the loss of moral restraint and the resulting violence seen than in the statistics of abortion. In the USA some note that the numbers of children aborted is declining. Yet the numbers show that at a rate of 1.3 million children a year are aborted. These innocent children, made in the image of God, never allowed to see the light of day. Their lives taken in the most violent ways. A generation that cries with alarm at dolphins caught in tuna nets, hardens their hearts and turns their backs as young children are sliced up alive and vacuumed out of wombs as so much waste to be discarded. Or in the case of older ones, in the procedures of 'partial birth' abortion, delivered until their head is out, and then holes drilled into their brains which are then sucked out. It is hard to imagine the brutality of these acts.

Do we go on to describe the cannibalizing of these children to describe the lack of moral restraint and the resulting violence? Not just the reports that come from China of aborted children that are smuggled to be eaten. Not just the aborted children who are used in skin products. But living children whose parts are taken to be used for others before they are put to death. Genetic research using these children as casually as one would go to an Auto parts store for parts for an automobile in need of repair. Is it any less cannibalizing of children to use them for resources for the living, then if we actually ate them? How the blood of these children cries out to God for judgment. How God is assuring them it will not be long before their blood is avenged. How arrogant and defiant of a society, whereas the Bible teaches no one has the right to take a life but God, we live in a world that says everyone has the right to take a life but God.

As we continue our survey of a generation that has lost its moral restraint, and see the resulting violence, we can spend much time on the entertainment world. Movies that seem to try and out do themselves in sexual grossness and raunchiness. Rap songs and artists that use the most debasing language toward women. Video games that feature graphic violence and women as sexual objects.

As the Bible describes a society in moral decline it seems that the public acceptance of homosexuality as a morally acceptable lifestyle is the last stage. Romans 1:24-32 clearly describes a society that has turned its collective back on God, and lost the moral restraint that a healthy fear of God brings. Why is the public moral acceptance of homosexuality the last stage of a society in moral decline? Is it that it is such a vile sin? The Bible teaches that sin is sin, and it is not that homosexuality is worse than other sins. It is because it turns the use of sexuality from the exact opposite of the reasons God has given to us this gift. It shows a society literally upside down from God's intent.

Romans 1:26-27 describes the issue of homosexuality this way. *"For this reason God gave them up to vile passions. For even their women exchanged the natural use for what is against nature. Likewise also the men, leaving the natural use of the woman, burned in their lust for one another, men with men committing what is shameful, and receiving in themselves the penalty of their errors which was due."* Homosexual desires and acts are totally upside down from God's creative purpose. It is not natural for men to burn in lust for men, and women to burn in lust for women. The male homosexual act is against nature, a violation of the body that brings it damage and diseases. It destroys God's creation of the family, a man and woman bearing and raising children.

It is true that homosexuality has always been part of society. It is unlikely that the percentage of people engaged has significantly increased. What is unique in a society in its last stages of moral decline, is when it is no longer kept in secret, but done in the open. What is unique is when it is no longer a sin condemned by society, but now a right that is accepted. God describes it this way in Romans 1:32 " . . . *who, knowing the righteous judgment of God, that those who practice such things are deserving of death, not only do the same but also approve of those who practice them."* It is a society absolutely upside down from God's intent that accepts as right homosexuality and its acts.

None of this justifies acts of violence against homosexuals. Acts of violence, discrimination are not how God would have one respond. The Christian is to treat all with love and respect. They are to view others as those who are trapped in sin, and need the love and grace of God to be delivered. But with this the Christian has the responsibility to clearly identify these lusts as sin, and these acts as abominations before God. Yet as society enters its last stage of the loss of moral restraint, it will reserve its anger and fury for those who would dare to call homosexuality a sin and unacceptable before God. We increasingly see this in the world today, as the anger and fury of society increasingly is evidenced against those who call it sin.

Where else do we go to describe a society in the last stages of the loss of moral restraint and the resulting violence? Do we describe the amazing and startling rise of slavery in this enlightened generation that prizes freedom? In Revelation 18 as the luxury trade of commercial Babylon (USA) is described it mentions in verse 13 trading in people, " . . . *and bodies and souls of men.*" How is it that an enlightened society traffics in people? Yet it is exactly the phenomena we see happening as the 21st century begins.

According to the United Nations the fastest growing business of organized crime is trafficking in people. They cite reliable estimates that 200 million people may now be in some way under the sway or in the hands of traffickers of various kinds worldwide. A comparison is drawn to the terrible days of slave trading in Africa. In four centuries of slave trading in Africa some 11.5 million people were moved out of Africa. Yet in the past decade 30 million women and children may have been trafficked within and from Southeast Asia for sexual purposes and sweatshop labor. It is estimated that a 100,000 Chinese pay to be smuggled overseas to Western countries every year. A Dallas newspaper reported that as many as 50,000 women and children from Asia, Latin America, and Eastern Europe are brought to the United States under false pretenses each year and forced to work as prostitutes, abused laborers or servants. One tragic result of the collapse of the Soviet Union has been the trafficking of women for prostitution.

Ironic, isn't it, that the last stage of the demand for freedom is the enslavement of others for the satisfaction of self. Ironic, isn't it, that the last stages of moral 'freedom' is enslavement to the lusts that now rule and enslave, as pornography so vividly demonstrates. Ironic, isn't it, that the last stages of the demand for moral freedom, leads to the greatest debasing of women and children we have known. Ironic, isn't it, that when all moral restraint is lost, no one is safe, no one is really free.

It should not surprise us that in the last stage of the loss of moral restraint, that the violence expressed is most clearly directed at Christians who stand for God and what is right. No group has known more violence as the 21$^{st}$ century begins than those who bear the Name of Jesus. There have been more people martyred for their faith in the Lord Jesus Christ in the last fifty years than have been martyred altogether in the centuries before. Human rights abuses of Christians lead all other abuses, yet the world is strangely silent. In country after country hostility, hatred, and violence toward Christians is on the rise. In nations reading like a roster of the United Nations; Indonesia, China, India, Sri Lanka, Pakistan, North Korea, Saudi Arabia, Sudan, Colombia, and the list goes on. Increasingly in the USA, a nation established for the freedom of religion, there is hostility toward Christians. A Christian morality that was once embraced, now rejected and increasingly viewed with hostility. Yet none of this should be surprising, for it is just as Jesus described. He says in Matthew 24:8-9, *"All these are the beginning of sorrows. Then they will deliver you up to tribulation and kill you, and you will be hated by all nations for My name's sake."*

The second way this generation is like the generation of Noah, is that it lives with no sense of the soon coming of the judgment of God. As Jesus describes their activity in Matthew 24:38-39, it is not so much their wickedness He emphasizes, but that to the very day judgment came they went about in the routines of daily life. He says, *"For as in the days before the flood, they were eating and drinking, marrying and giving in marriage, until the day that Noah entered the ark, and did not know until the flood came and took them all away, so also will the coming of the Son of Man be."* So it is today.

We see even today a Christian world that tends to put down those who talk of coming judgment and the return of the Lord Jesus Christ. A generation that has seen the greatest amount of fulfilled prophecy in the news of the day since the time of Jesus, either ignoring or ignorant of the evidence all around them. But even the sleeping nature of the church, and the rejection of those who point to the soon return of the Lord Jesus Christ is an evidence of our times. As the Bible says in 2 Peter 3:3, *" knowing this first; that scoffers will come in the last days, walking according to their own lusts, and saying, "Where is the promise of His coming? For since the fathers fell asleep, all things continue as they were from the beginning of creation."*

Ultimately though this truth is not about a world, even a Christian world. Ultimately this is all about you. Are you most like a Noah type generation, or most like a Noah? Noah was known as a man who walked in righteousness. It was said of Noah in Genesis 6:8-9, *"But Noah found grace in the eyes of the Lord. This is the genealogy of Noah. Noah was a just man, perfect in his generations. Noah walked with God."* What simple, yet profound statements to be made about a man. He found grace in the eyes of the Lord. He walked with God. Noah was not perfect in an absolute sense, only Jesus has been the perfect man. But Noah pursued righteousness. He didn't use the immorality of his day as an excuse for himself. He turned his back on that immorality so he could walk with God. This book, this moment is the chance for you to examine your life before God. No matter where you have walked, what immorality you have pursued, you can find grace in the eyes of the Lord. Turn from your sins, and turn to the call of God to you through the Lord Jesus Christ. Turn from compromise, to the wonderful life of walking with God. It's not too late for you. Make this day the decisive moment in your life and eternity.

# 19 | The Day of Peace (Not!)

*"For when they say, "Peace and safety!" then sudden destruction comes upon them, as labor pains upon a pregnant woman. And they shall not escape.*
1 Thessalonians 5:3

How does it happen? How does the world enter this final seven-year period, called the Great Tribulation, that ends with the return of the Lord Jesus Christ to establish His kingdom on earth? We have seen all the elements in place. Israel miraculously returned to the nations of the world. Israel in control of Jerusalem as its capital, yet in times of great trouble. A loose coalition of 'merchants' working with political, academic, media leaders toward a world in which nation states loose their significance, religions loose their sense of distinctives, a global economy the unifying force in the world. Europe moving toward political, economic, military union. The USA as the economic giant whose success and lust for luxury brings prosperity to the merchants and political leaders, 'rulers', of the other nations. The focus of the merchants and political leaders to bring a peaceful resolution to Israel and its Arab nations, so that the economy has hope for stability.

Jesus, and the Bible, indicate that in the last stages of time, as the world moves toward its unifying in the final rebellion against God, and His rule through His Son the Lord Jesus Christ, the true church becomes the increasing focus of the hatred and scorn of the world. As we saw in the last chapter, Jesus describing in Matthew 24:9-13, the rise of persecution of those who uphold Jesus in spirit and truth. The rise of false teachers, who corrupt the truth of God to satisfy the lusts and sinful appetites of people. A rise of spirituality generally in the world, but only a form of godliness, not the real thing. The realization of many that those who uphold Jesus in spirit and truth are the enemies of the oneness the world seeks. The claim to Jesus as the exclusive truth of God infuriates. The unwillingness to compromise morally, particularly in the lustful, perverse sexual expressions of the last days. The fight against the slaughter of young children in their mother's wombs, and the definition of abortion as murder, enraging those who want to decide for themselves what child lives, what child dies. All of these increasingly isolate true disciples of the Lord Jesus Christ, and bring increasing fury and a desire to silence or eliminate. All of this making it seem as if it is these followers of Jesus who are keeping the world from the new day, the new order that will bring peace and prosperity that is secure. As this hostility to followers of Jesus rises, there is also a rising hope for peace talks with Israel. It is then that a surprising event happens, that at first shocks the world, but soon brings a rising sense of celebration.

The promise that Jesus gave His church is that He would come back for her, and He does. The promise He would keep her from the seven years of tribulation coming to the world (Luke 21:36, Revelation 3:10, Revelation 4:1), and He will. The promise that in a moment, in the twinkling of an eye He would snatch His bride from the danger of the hour. As we have seen, 1 Thessalonians 4:13-17 describes the moment. Jesus comes from heaven with those with living faith in Him, who have passed through death. As Jesus waits in the air, they come to earth, stand up beside those living by faith in Christ. At that instant the bodies of Christians are all transformed into a likeness of the body of Jesus. Maintaining their distinctness, but gaining a body no longer operating by the principle of blood, now by the principle of spirit. As 1 Corinthians 15:42-44 describes, *"So also is the resurrection of the dead. The body is sown in corruption, it is raised in incorruption. It is sown in dishonor, it is raised in glory. It is sown in weakness, it is raised in power. It is sown a natural body, it is raised a spiritual body."* Also, raised with them are the children of believing Christians who have not reached the age of accountability. As 1 Corinthians 7:14 promises the children of believers are seen as holy in the site of God until they are old enough to make their own decisions for or against Jesus, *"For the unbelieving husband is sanctified by the wife, and the unbe- · lieving wife is sanctified by the husband; otherwise your children would be unclean, but now they are holy."*

Jesus said no one would know the day or the hour that the Rapture, the snatching off earth just before the night of the Tribulation, comes. As we have discussed, though, every major event in Jesus' life has happened on the corresponding holy day given by the Lord in the feasts of Israel. In sequence and in exact fulfillment Jesus has fulfilled the promise given by God. The next in sequence of being fulfilled is Rosh Hashana, the Feast of Trumpets. This is a two-day feast marked by great celebration. Trumpets are blown one hundred times over the two days. Each day ends with one last, long sound of the trumpet. 1 Corinthians 15:51-52 describes the coming of Jesus for His bride, the church, this way, *"Behold, I tell you a mystery: We shall not all sleep, but we shall all be changed—in a moment, in the twinkling of an eye, at the last trumpet. For the trumpet will sound, and the dead will be raised incorruptible, and we shall be changed."* As Jesus said, He would come at the sounding of the last trumpet. Thus some early Fall, soon, on one of those two days, at one of the hours, the trumpet will sound in Israel, only this time in a moment the eye cannot capture, every true believer in Jesus Christ, and their children, are taken off earth to meet the Lord in the air.

What does the world say? Suddenly thousands of Christians at once are missing. No trace can be found. Sadly, Jesus indicated, it will not be as many in number as we might think and hope. Jesus warns of many in the last days, who believe they are Christians and are not. Many who find that day not to be a release but a trap. Where will you be that day? Do you have a life that evidences the call of Jesus to take up the Cross and follow Him? These are the days to be sure. At that moment there will be no escape from the night of judgment that is coming. Jesus describes people living, working side by side, but one is taken and one is left. His words in Matthew 24:40-41, *"Then two men will be in the field: one will be taken and the other left. Two women will be grinding at the mill: one will be taken and the other left."* How surprising it will be to the many who truly are left behind.

What does the world say? This is speculation, but it seems that the response is likely in two stages. First, there will be shock. It will be unfiltered. There will be much discussion about the Rapture, judgment, end times, and Christians who believed who are now missing. But I think that will quickly end. Soon the media will be spinning a story of celebration. There will be a sense of good riddance. A sense that for the world to evolve to the new day of peace, these needed to be gone. It is possible that already stories are prepared to explain in a positive way the troubling thoughts and questions that come from thousands suddenly missing. We know in Jesus' day, the religious leaders were preparing a cover story for the Ressurection even before it happened. They were already developing a strategy to explain away the Ressurection (Matthew 27:62-66). We know that when news of Jesus' Ressurection was known to them, they quickly developed a 'story' to explain His missing body as only a plot of His cult (Matthew 28:11-15). Whether it is in a story developed in advance, or one developed in response, the media will soon spin a story that brings, if not explanation, at least a call for celebration and promise for what a new day without them will bring. Many 'Christian' leaders will come forward to assure the world that if true Christians were taken, they would have been taken as well.

The Bible describes that the disappearance of many will not be a long running story, for news will be quickly taken over by the talks with Israel, and the promise of peace. Following the sequence of the feast of Israel, ten days after Rosh Hashana, is the Day of Atonement, Yom Kippur. The Day of Atonement is the beginning of the night of judgment to the world, but it is the promise of salvation to Israel. As we will see in the next chapter, the long night of judgment of Israel as a nation is over. In the promise of Isaiah 40:1,2, her sins are atoned for, and now the day of salvation through the Messiah, the Lord Jesus Christ, has come.

For Satan, the disappearance of the church, brings the opportunity for which he has long sought. The moment to bring his leader to world dominance. The moment to lead the nations in defiance of God. Satan still believing that he can defeat God. Satan believing he can keep Jesus from the throne as King of Kings. That he can keep the everlasting kingdom of righteousness from coming to earth. Satan is the ultimate egotist, who not till the end, believes he will lose. As Daniel 7:25 says, he inspires his earthly puppet, the Antichrist, to believe that, " . . . *And shall intend to change times and law . . .".* Satan believes he can change the times and law that God has decreed.

With the church gone, all restraint on Satan and his plans is removed. Satan has had many efforts to bring his man to world domination. Hitler was only the latest of many attempts. But God has kept thwarting him through the work of the Holy Spirit, working to restrain evil through the lives and the influence of the followers of the Lord Jesus Christ. Now they are gone. 2 Thessalonians 2:7-8 describes the results, *"For the mystery of lawlessness is already at work; only He who now restrains will do so until He is taken out of the way. And then the lawless one will be revealed, whom the Lord will consume with the breath of His mouth and destroy with the brightness of His coming."* The Bible does not say the Holy Spirit is taken off of earth, for He will remain active until the end. What it does say is that His restraining influence is removed. With all true followers of the Lord Jesus Christ gone, Satan has almost free reign to bring his long desired plan to become reality.

The news of the disappearance of thousands is soon replaced with the trumpeting of peace. A leader from the world of Europe and the USA has negotiated a peace treaty with Israel and its neighbors. The thorny, seeming impossible issues between Israel, the Palestinians, and its Arab neighbors are resolved. A seven-year peace treaty is signed, and how appropriate that its beginning corresponds with Israel's most holy day, Yom Kippur (Daniel 9:27). A world celebrates with the news, and as 1 Thessalonians 5:3 says they begin to believe that *"Peace and safety!"*, have come in the most serious issue that threatens world peace.

The elements of the treaty can be known from God's Word, and inferences that can be easily made. It is guaranteed by the nations of Europe, perhaps through NATO, or the United Nations. Israel disarms, as it dwells in what Ezekiel 38:11 describes as, " . . . *a land of unwalled villages; I will go to a peaceful people, who dwell safely, all of them dwelling without walls, and having neither bars nor gates."* It is likely that Jerusalem is internationalized in a way that allows the major religions to have their religious sites. We know that at some point before the middle of the treaty, the three and a half year point, Jerusalem has a Temple built for the Jewish people. This aspect of the treaty is likely to be used by the leader of the Roman Catholic church, representing Christianity, to lead the leaders of Islam in celebrating this answer to the puzzle of how to bring peace when all three major religions claim Jerusalem as a holy site. We will meet the key man who brings this about more clearly in the next chapter, but as celebrated as the peace treaty is, so also is the man who is instrumental in bringing it about. This man is seen as a man of destiny who has the skills to lead the world to peace and prosperity. A man who seems ambitious for peace and prosperity, not for himself. But all that soon changes.

All of these events are in process as I write. From the world's perspective these are just ordinary, hopeful events. Apart from the disappearance of the followers of the Lord Jesus Christ, nothing extraordinary has happened. Analysts have been talking about peace in the Mideast for the more than fifty years of modern Israel's existence. The Antichrist does not come with horns and cape. He is just an ordinary, pragmatic politician, who finds his personal destiny and desires being defined by the opportunity to bring peace to the world. It is a scenario that the merchants have been working toward for the years since World War 2. It has been phased and coordinated. The development of the European Union and Japan, to counter balance the enormous power and wealth of the USA. The diminishing of nation states, and the rise of worldwide corporations and a global economy. The diminishing of religious distinctives and the moving toward a common sense that each are about the same thing, and thus they are all more alike than they are different.

Let's see in the next chapter how things develop. But let us not make this speculation and debate. Ultimately this moment will define you, and who you truly are. It is likely that some of you will be reading this after these events are in process. Let me encourage you that the last chapter is for you. It's not too late, for God is full of mercy, and the door through Jesus is open for you.

# 20 | The Day of Atonement

*""Comfort, yes, comfort My people!" says your God. "Speak comfort to Jerusalem and cry out to her, that her warfare is ended, that her iniquity is pardoned; for she has received from the Lord's hand double from the Lord for all her sins."""*
Isaiah 40:1-2

What's the purpose of this seven-year period of the Tribulation? Why doesn't God just end things? His purposes are twofold. One is to judge the nations. By Satan raising up a man, the Antichrist who clearly defines and expresses the rebellion of man against God, the justice of God in judgment is demonstrated. The second purpose is the concluding part of a great love story. God, by His own purposes and will, has set a special love on the Jewish people and Jerusalem. It is at many points a tragic love story, for again and again Israel is unfaithful to God. God though loves with an amazing love. He made a promise to Abraham, and renewed it to Isaac and Jacob. He promised He would bring a kingdom to earth, centered in Jerusalem, for Abraham and his descendants. The seven years of the Tribulation is about God calling from the last generation of the Jewish people, a people who will receive Jesus as Messiah, Savior, and Lord. It is about the nation of Israel lovingly and eagerly welcoming the Lord Jesus to bring the kingdom to earth at the end of the Tribulation.

With true followers of Jesus Christ gone, and the peace treaty in effect, everything to the world seems to be perfect. A great rise of optimism, and a time of worldwide peace sweeps the world. Suddenly all things seem possible. Then there appear two men in Jerusalem who become the sole disruptive, corrupting force of this euphoria the world feels. All seems moving to oneness. Oneness among nations, oneness among religions. If peace can be found in Jerusalem among the deeply divisive people and religious issues that have divided that land throughout its history, then it is possible for a world. These two men proclaim a truth that again infuriates all, they say that Jesus is Messiah, Savior, and Lord. They say only in Jesus Christ can one have peace with God, forgiveness of sin, and acceptance into the kingdom of God. The official church from Rome castigates them. Some leaders of Judaism in Jerusalem furiously put down the two men and their message.

Who are these two men? The Bible describes them in Revelation 11:3-6, "*And I will give power to my two witnesses, and they will prophesy one thousand two hundred and sixty days clothed in sackcloth. These are the two olive trees and the two lampstands standing before the God of the earth. And if anyone wants to harm them, fire proceeds from their mouth and devours their enemies. And if anyone wants to harm them, he must be killed in this manner. These have power to shut heaven, so that no rain falls in the days of their prophecy; and they have power over waters to turn them to blood, and to strike the earth with all plagues as often as they desire.*"

These men come with a great similarity to the ministries of Moses and Elijah. Moses came to deliver the Israelites from slavery to Egypt. Moses was given power to bring plagues to the earth, like turning the water in the Nile to blood. Elijah came with a warning of judgment, and prayed it would not rain on the earth, and it did not rain for three and a half years. These two witnesses come with the exact same purposes, to call the Jewish people to salvation and to warn a world of the judgment of God.

Are these two witnesses Moses and Elijah? Many speculate that they are. When Jesus was transfigured in His life on earth, it was Moses and Elijah who appeared with him. Moses representing the law, Elijah representing the prophets. Other people believe it may be Enoch and Elijah. Enoch and Elijah never went through death. Enoch was taken to be with God. Elijah went away in a spectacular way in a chariot. While it is fun to speculate and debate, the truth is that nowhere does the Bible identify who these two witnesses are. Revelation just calls them the two witnesses in fulfillment of the prophecy of Zechariah 4:2-3,14. As Zechariah indicates, the significance is not in who the two men are, but that they prophesy in the power of the Holy Spirit, as Zechariah 4:6 states, *"Not by might, nor by power, but by My Spirit, says the Lord of hosts."*

These two men begin to witness of Jesus to the Jewish people, and to warn the nations of the world of the judgment of God. Since the church is gone, they are the living witnesses on earth of Jesus as Messiah, Savior, and Lord. They prophesy that it will not rain, and it does not rain during the three and a half years of their time of prophesying. They begin to pronounce plagues on the earth as the judgment of God begins on the nations. The world enraged, tries to silence them. But they cannot. They try to seize them, but the witnesses call down fire to destroy those who would take them.

In Israel people begin to respond. They step forward to pronounce their faith in Jesus Christ, as Messiah, Savior, and Lord. Their number grows. Revelation 7:1-8 describes 144,000 of them professing faith in Jesus. The worst judgments to earth are held off until the full number of them are sealed as believers in the Lord Jesus Christ. Revelation 14:4 describes them as virgins. While that is possible in the physical sense, what is most likely meant is that they are virgins spiritually. They have committed their lives to Jesus. They are as the apostle Paul describes in 2 Corinthians 11:1, *"For I am jealous for you with godly jealousy.*

*For I have betrothed you to one husband, that I may present you as a chaste virgin to Christ."*

In addition to those saved among the Jewish people by these two witnesses in Jerusalem, it is also obvious that a number of people around the world come to saving faith in Jesus. While many are deceived and fall for the false forms of Christianity and religions of the world being offered, not all are. As Christians have disappeared, as the two witnesses in Jerusalem have world-wide attention as they proclaim Jesus as Messiah, Savior, and Lord; many are listening. These become the Tribulation saints mentioned in Revelation. The Holy Spirit is still actively at work. Some may be those who have been witnessed to by family or friends. They may read the Bible to try and understand what is happening. They may read books like this that help them understand what is going on, and who Jesus is. They pay a price for their faith in the last three and a half years. Many put in prison. Many killed. However, nothing they suffer in this life can compare to the eternity with God they have gained, and the eternity in the fires of hell they have escaped. These are part of the reason Revelation is written with such detail given of these seven years. Revelation will become their survival guide, as parts of it speak directly to them (Revelation 13:8-10, 14:12-13).

While these two witnesses are proclaiming Jesus as Savior, Lord, Messiah, in Jerusalem, things also are developing around the man who has seemingly gained peace for the world. The leader who has secured the peace treaty with Israel is increasingly seen as a man of destiny. In a vacuum of leadership he is stepping forward with great popularity. He comes out of the leadership in Europe. Ten key nations in Europe form the core of the power base. This man emerges taking over from three of the ten, as described in Daniel 7:8. His intent to dominate the world himself is not immediately apparent. He appears to be a man of peace.

He dramatically captures the world's attention when he is the subject of an assassination attempt. Revelation carefully describes what happens in Revelation 13:3, *"And I saw one of his heads as if it had been mortally wounded, and his deadly wound was healed. And all the world marveled and followed the beast."* To the world it looks like this leader has been struck dead. A head wound that no one could recover from. The leader of the false church in Rome, the Pope of that day, ministers to him. It appears to be a resurrection-like miracle, for the leader is dramatically healed. Not only did he not die, he recovers as one full of life. The world marvels at this recovery, and the religious power that has enabled him to recover. They see this as evidence that destiny has laid its hand upon this man. He is perceived to have supernatural powers. Those who have been moving the world to a one world order now have their man to rally behind. The final act in the great drama is about to unfold.

All of this is reflective of Satan as the great imitator. Just as God's man, Jesus, was killed and then resurrected, Satan offers his substitute in the same way. While Jesus did die and rise to life, the Antichrist is a fraud. He only appears to have suffered a fatal head wound, and then recover. Only God is Lord of life. Satan can cause the body to be killed, but only God can bring the dead to life. This delusion, though, impresses many.

The recovery from a seemingly fatal head wound by this world leader is part of a demonstration of power by the leader of the false church in Rome. Revelation 13:13 describes the spectacular seeming evidences of power, *"He performs great signs, so that he even makes fire come down from heaven on the earth in the sight of men."* The false prophet leads what the Bible calls the great apostasy, the great falling away from true faith in the Lord Jesus Christ. The world forgets that even the false priests of Egypt could duplicate many of the miracles done by Moses. Satan has limited power. In contrast to the true witness of Jesus offered by the two witnesses in Jerusalem, he brings a false witness. The world is persuaded by the seeming powers of this man and religion. 2 Thessalonians 2:9-12 describes how many fall for this final and eternally fatal lie, *"The coming of the lawless one is according to the working of Satan with all power, signs, and lying wonders, and with all unrighteous deception among those who perish, because they did not receive the love of the truth, that they might be saved. And for this reason God will send them strong delusion, that they should believe the lie, that they all may be condemned who did not believe the truth but had pleasure in unrighteousness."* Interesting, isn't it, that they believe the lie not because of the powers and signs they see, but because they first had decided they would rather have sin than God. They believed the lie because they didn't want the truth. The rejection of the truth came first. The lie just gives the convenient way to embrace sin, yet still seem to be religious. That is why it is so important in your life that you understand the call of God in Jesus Christ to repent and turn from sin, and self rule; to take up a cross and to follow Jesus.

While the world focuses on this man, the two witnesses in Jerusalem continue to bring their witness of Jesus. They pronounce plagues, judgments from God, and they start to come. The four horsemen of conquering, war, famine, death begin to ride in full fury. Great persecution and martyrdom of the new believers in Jesus erupt around the world. The world cannot touch the two witnesses in Jerusalem, so their fury turns on those who believe in the Jesus they proclaim. Terrifying and devastating judgments come from God. A third of the green and living plants are destroyed. Something strikes the oceans, perhaps a meteor, and waters turn to blood, a third of the ships are destroyed. Rivers become contaminated and the water undrinkable. Clouds of dust from the meteors rise up and is so thick a third of the sunlight is lost during the day, and the dust and smoke obscures the moon and stars at night. War with chemical weapons breaks out. A third of mankind dies. And all this is only the beginning and the milder parts of the terror that is to come in the last three and a half years.

In the next chapter we will see the key changes that come at the midpoint of the seven-year period. The remarkable death and resurrection of the two witnesses. Satan thrown out of heaven, coming to earth in a fury. The man of peace declared to be a god to be worshiped. But it is well to pause again and to be sure you have understood and responded to the call of the Lord Jesus Christ to turn from and repent of sin, and to turn in faith to Jesus as your Savior and Lord. This is the day of salvation, the Bible says. It is always today. Be sure that this day your life rests by faith in the Lord Jesus Christ.

# 21 | The Day of the Beast

> *"So the great dragon was cast out, that serpent of old,*
> *called the Devil and Satan, who deceives the whole world;*
> *he was cast to the earth and his angels were cast out with*
> *him."*
> Revelation 12:9

It is at the middle of the seven-year period that literally all hell breaks loose. The most significant event happens not on earth, but in heaven. Satan, who over created time has had access to the presence of God, is finally and eternally cast out from heaven. It would be well to spend a little time on this part of the story. Much of it filled with mystery, yet with enough detail to provide a lot of information. Who is Satan, or the Devil, as the names are used interchangeably? Where did he and evil come from?

The Bible provides information in some detail on Satan in Isaiah 14 and Ezekiel 28. In Isaiah 14:12 he is called Lucifer, son of the morning. In Ezekiel 28 he is called the anointed cherub over the earth. Satan was a part of a class of heavenly beings created to serve God. Satan was among the highest, and he was given responsibility over the earth before man was created. He was created in innocence by God, but created with will. God has always sought service to Him that is rooted in love and honor. For love to be real there must be the choice to love or not to love. Satan became obsessed with pride. Carried away by his own beauty, he was content no longer to serve God. He wanted the place of God. He led a rebellion against the rule of God. Revelation 12:4 indicated that he led about a third of the angels in rebellion against God. In the violent war against God it appears that earth was severely damaged. The phrase in Genesis 1:2 describing the earth as without form and void, is used to indicate something that has been ruined. It may be why we see such conflicting evidence in the earth of apparent great age, and yet in many ways young.

Following the rebellion and defeat, Satan was given limited freedom. We meet him in the Bible first in the garden in Genesis 3 tempting Eve and Adam. We see him in Job having access to the presence of God. Satan seems to be making the case before God that no one serves God out of love and honor, but only out of self-interest. When God calls attention to the love and honor that Job brings to the Lord, Satan indicates it is only because of all the ways he is blessed. Take away the blessing and Job would curse God. Job does lose all the evidences of 'blessing' in his life, and he does remain faithful to God. We see that God is using Satan to establish His worth and glory as God works His will on earth. Ephesians 3:8-12 states that God is demonstrating to the created heavenly beings His greatness and the wisdom of His plans by His work through the church in this life.

While Satan was defeated in his plan to take the throne from God, he has never given up the desire and the fight. As we said earlier, Satan is the ultimate egotist who is still seeking to win. Mankind has become his proxy in the battle against God. The world leader of the Tribulation, the Antichrist becomes his substitute for Jesus. Rome his substitute for Israel. The events of the Tribulation are the last stages in this dramatic conflict.

At the exact midpoint of the seven years Satan is finally removed from heaven. He is cast to earth as Revelation 12:9 states. He comes to earth furious, and in some ways in panic. He knows his time is short. He knows God plans to bring Jesus to earth as

King of Kings, and Lord of Lords. He comes to bring his last, best effort to keep Jesus from the rule of the nations.

Just before Satan is thrown out, in fact three and a half days before he is, the two witnesses of Jesus in Jerusalem have completed their ministry on earth. The 144,000 Jewish believers in Jesus as Messiah, Savior, and Lord are sealed. The two witnesses have had God's special protective care and nothing will touch them from the judgments and plagues to come, or from the hatred and hostility of Satan and the Antichrist. As their ministry ends, so does the protective care they have been under. The pits of hell seem to prevail as they are killed. The occasion of their death causes the world to throw a party. They do not bury them, but leave their bodies dead in the street, the pictures of them broadcast around the world. Revelation 11:9-10 describes the world seeing their bodies and its response, *"Then those from the peoples, tribes, tongues, and nations will see their dead bodies three and a half days, and not allow their dead bodies to be put into graves. And those who dwell on the earth will rejoice over them, make merry, and send gifts to one another, because these two prophets tormented those who dwell on the earth."* The world thinks that if they are dead, than the world has won and the judgments will end, since the messengers of God's judgement are dead.

However, the party is short lived. After three and a half days they are resurrected to life before the eyes of the world. A voice is heard calling them up to heaven. In an event witnessed globally through television and Internet, they rise to heaven in a most dramatic fashion. At the same time a devastating earthquake hits Jerusalem and seven thousand people are killed.

At this point the fury of Satan is turned against those who have come to faith in Jesus, who are the Jewish believers in Israel. But God protects and takes them to a place prepared for them in the wilderness. Revelation 12:13-17 describes the events. They are taken by air. Many believe to a place called Petra, a fortress city in southern Jordan. Petra is a whole city built into a canyon so narrow, that it is barely wider than a horse going in. Satan tries to destroy them but God stops him. These 144,000 represent the nation of Israel who will be kept safe in this place until the three and a half years are completed. They will welcome Jesus to earth as the Messiah of Israel comes to bring the promised kingdom of God to earth. Satan unable to destroy these believers in Jesus, turns his fury to those others who have faith in Jesus around the world. Revelation 12:17 describes it this way, *"And the dragon was enraged with the woman, and he went to make war with the rest of her offspring, who keep the commandments of God and have the testimony of Jesus Christ."* It is to these saints that much of Revelation is written to give them encouragement to remain faithful to Jesus, even at the expense of freedom and loss of life.

The death and resurrection of the two witnesses is not the only interesting event that takes place in Jerusalem at this time. Satan and the Antichrist bring the final act to the strategy they have developed. It is now that this man of peace seizes the moment and declares himself to be a god. An image of this man is placed in the rebuilt Temple of Israel in Jerusalem. With the leader of the false church in Rome, the Pope, being the spokesman, he is declared to be a god to be worshiped, obeyed, followed. He declares himself against the God of heaven. Revelation 13:6-8 describes this happening, *"Then he opened his mouth in blasphemy against God, to blaspheme His name, His tabernacle, and those who dwell in heaven. It was granted to him to make war with the saints and to overcome them. And authority was given to him over every tribe, tongue, and nation. All who dwell on the earth will worship him, whose names have not been written in the Book of Life of the Lamb slain from the foundation of the world."*

The Antichrist gains his position of world rule from three sources. One is the religious leader of the false church in Rome. He is the prophet of this new 'god', calling people to worship him. Creating and endorsing a seeming living image of the Antichrist in the temple in Jerusalem. He institutes the system in which no one can buy or sell anything without the mark that indicates their allegiance to the Antichrist. It says they receive the mark on their forehead or right hand. We know from technology being used to day it is possible to place a computer chip as small as a piece of rice under the skin that could be computer read. Already in Los Angeles this is used with dogs and cats so that if they are found their owners can be quickly identified.

A second source of the Antichrist position of power is his seeming miraculous comeback from death, when he had the apparently fatal head wound. This adds great credibility to his claim to deity. A third source of his power is rather interesting. It is a group of ten world leaders who have no current position of power. Read how Revelation 17:12-13 describes them, *"The ten horns which you saw are ten kings who have received no kingdom as yet, but they receive authority for one hour as kings with the beast. These are of one mind, and they will give their power and authority to the beast."* This council of ten appears to be former leaders of governments, Presidents, Prime Ministers, who convince the world that there should be a superseding government, with the Antichrist as head, that leads the world. They are part of the conspiracy of the merchants mentioned in Revelation 18:23, that have been working since World War 2 to a one world government that will bring peace to the world, so that the global markets are stable and profit is maximized. Their intent was economic, not spiritual partners with Satan. But what they have done becomes the tools that Satan uses to fulfill his purposes. Like all who fall for Satan's lies, in the end they are only fools who are destroyed. It is at this time that the great tragedy of the USA, once the nation that sent so many Gospel witnesses around the world, now endorses and supports the imprisonment and killing of those who believe in the Lord Jesus Christ.

A lot happens in these few days at the midpoint of the seven years. A lot more is yet to happen. In the next chapter we will see the worldwide coalition soon fall apart. We will see the final and terrifying unleashing of the judgments of God on earth. We will see the long desired and eagerly awaited return of the Lord Jesus Christ in glory and fierce power. How important it is to be sure our allegiance is to Jesus Christ and His kingdom. Make sure your life is about intimately knowing Him and passionately following Him. All kingdoms fall but the one that Jesus builds.

# 22 | The Day of Armageddon

*"Let the nations be wakened, and come to the Valley of Jehoshaphat, For there I will sit to judge all the surrounding nations. Put in the sickle, for the harvest is ripe. Come, go down; for the winepress is full, the vats overflow—for their wickedness is great."*
Joel 3:12-12

The world appears at the midpoint of the seven years of the Tribulation as if everything Satan has wanted is accomplished. His substitute for Jesus has been crowned as king and lord in Jerusalem. All the nations of the world have joined in supporting him as the supreme world ruler. The religions of the world, led by the Pope and the church centered in Rome, are in worship of him. Satan is seen as the true and right power of god. The last witnesses of Jesus, apart from the 144,000 are being imprisoned and silenced. The ultimate global economy has been established. No one can buy or sell without the mark of worship of the Antichrist. The two witnesses of Jesus and their prophetic powers have left earth. All should be well. Yet it is only illusions. Soon a whirl of events will leave all of what Satan has established in ruins and ashes. Soon Jesus will be received and crowned on earth as King of Kings and Lord of Lords.

The Bible says that only in Jesus will the world know true and lasting peace and unity. It compares the wicked to the ocean, always restless, always moving, knowing no peace. Isaiah 57:20-21 describes this truth, *"But the wicked are like the troubled sea, when it cannot rest, whose waters cast up mire and dirt. "There is no peace", says my God, "for the wicked."* And, just as God has said, no sooner has the worldwide unity that Satan has sought through the Antichrist gained, as it is just as soon lost. The global economy the merchants have been working for a generation to achieve through political and religious unity, falls apart with terrifying swiftness and devastating loss of life.

Once the rulers of the world see the true agenda of the Antichrist, personal aggrandizement of power and control, then the coalition begins to fall apart. The first to break from the unity is Asia, led by China. China, fielding a modern army of two hundred million comes against Israel from the East. Since the Antichrist has taken Jerusalem and the temple as his place of worship and center of power, the battles will take place in the land of Israel. We know that right now Turkey has dammed the Euphrates river. The river is a barrier to the east of Israel. Turkey now could totally dam up the river, and that is what happens as China advances. The armies that come from the East have their colors described as red, yellow, and blue. We know that historically yellow has been the color of the Emperors of China, red has been the color of the nation of China, blue the color of the ruling class of China. Imagine the destruction and devastation that will come from a fully equipped army of two hundred million coming to do battle in an area of land as small as Israel is.

As China comes, and a series of other armies follow to battle the Antichrist, the battles take place in an area of Israel called Armageddon. Armageddon comes from the combination of two Hebrew words, the word for hills or mountains, and the name of the city Megiddo. Thus, Armageddon is the region around Megiddo. Megiddo was an important city in Israel's past. Israel was the key land bridge for trade between the East and the West. The trade route would pass through the beautiful valley in Northern Israel that bends around, almost banana shaped, from the Mediterranean to the Jordan River. Megiddo was the key fortress city in the valley (the valley in the Bible is called Jezreel). Whoever controlled Megiddo controlled the trade route. That is why Israel was such a desired spot in the world in biblical times, and why so many of the world powers sought to control it. As history comes to its end this area resumes its importance. It gains importance not because of trade routes, but because it is the land the Antichrist has established for his worship in the world.

As the armies come against the Antichrist, beginning with the Chinese, the battles are fought in the region around Megiddo, or Armageddon. When the Bible describes the battle of Armageddon, it is not describing one battle, but a series of wars that come like waves crashing against the shore. The first are the Chinese, but more follow. As these battles go on, the bloodshed is so great, the Bible describes the blood flowing in the valley as high as the bridle of a horse. Listen to the words of Revelation 14:20 describing this, *"And the winepress was trampled outside the city, and blood came out of the winepresses, up to the horses' bridles, for one thousand six hundred furlongs."* How sobering to consider the terrible consequences of the rebellion against God.

Following the armies of the East coming against the Antichrist in Armageddon, the next armies to come is a coalition led by Russia. Ezekiel 38 describes this in a lot of detail. The prophet describes a coalition made up of Russia, Iran, Ethiopia, and Libya. Their plan comes as a total surprise to the Antichrist. But what is most surprising is who they take out first. The great power behind the Antichrist and the global economic, religious, and political unity has been the USA. The power of their economy and the power of their military has been in full support. Russia cannot successfully seize the wealth of the Mideast, the oil resources, unless the power of the USA is neutralized. It is then that a totally unsuspecting nation and world, see its destruction in one hour's time.

Revelation 18:8 describes the destruction of the USA, *"Therefore her plagues will come in one day—death and mourning and famine. And she will be utterly burned with fire, for strong is the Lord God who judges her."* Jeremiah 50-51 also describe the destruction of the USA. It indicates its destruction comes from the North, in a plot coordinated with Iran. Russia, which has not destroyed its nuclear warheads and missiles, unleashes a devastating nuclear attack on the USA. It is from North to South, East to West, and nothing survives. Revelation 18 describes the ships of the sea seeing the USA burn, and remarks that in one hour such a great nation came to its end. Though this destruction came by the hand of Russia, Iran, and the coalition with them, the judgment of the USA was from God.

With the USA out of the way, Russia and its allies move on the land of Israel. Sweeping down with their armies they expect to have an easy victory. However, this plan is also part of the judgment of God. For there, as part of the battles of Armageddon, Russia and its coalition meet its defeat. As fire is mentioned in its defeat and judgment, it is likely that nuclear weapons are used against it as well.

While these battles are going on, the news of the terrible losses in the area of Armageddon is not the only upsetting news in the world. God is also increasing the fury and amount of His judgment on the world. Those not affected by the battles in Armageddon, or the nuclear destruction of the USA, will certainly be ravaged by the direct judgments of God. The seven last judgments, described as the bowls of God's wrath, come upon the earth. A painful plague of sores that come upon mankind. All of the oceans becoming like blood, and all the creatures that live in the sea dying. All of the fresh water springs and rivers turning to blood, and becoming undrinkable. All of the protective covering from the sun being lost, and the heat and scorching power of the sun blistering all. A time of darkness that comes over the earth, so thick a person cannot see even his or her own hand. The Euphrates dried up so the armies of the East can freely come.

The battles of Armageddon bring their terrible loss of life. Finally, a worldwide earthquake so significant it levels mountains and eliminates the islands of the sea. How terrifying is the judgment of God, stored up against the rebellion of man over the generations.

As these events happen, even the Antichrist's own inner circle cannot stay united. In an irony that is cruel, yet inevitable, the Antichrist and his political leaders turn on the false church and religious leaders. The religious leaders have been pawns of the political leaders, and the political leaders take delight in destroying them once they are no longer needed to gain power. The ten leaders who have given their allegiance to the Antichrist take delight in the destruction of the leader of the false church in Rome. Revelation 18:16 describes it this way, *"And the ten horns which you saw on the beast, these will hate the harlot, make her desolate and naked, eat her flesh and burn her with fire."*

The last chapter and statement in the story, though, belongs not to man, but to God. Just as the last word in your life will not be yours or anybody else's, but God's. When Jesus went to Jerusalem for the last time before the Cross, He came in riding on a young colt. That He came that way was very significant. When a king came to a city, he indicated his intent by the kind of horse he rode. If he came on a young colt, he was indicating that he came in peace. If he came on a mighty horse, he was indicating he was coming to conquer by force. Jesus, the first time comes to Jerusalem on a colt, indicated He was coming offering peace to all who would welcome Him as Messiah, Savior, Lord and King. The next time Jesus comes to Jerusalem it will not be on a young colt offering peace, He will come on a mighty horse with the armies of heaven, to conquer by force. Read as Revelation 19:11-16 describes Him as He comes, *"Now I saw heaven opened, and behold a white horse. And He who sat on him was called Faithful and True, and in righteousness He judges and makes war. His eyes were like a flame of fire, and on His head were many crowns. He had a name written that no one knew except Himself. He was clothed with a robe dipped in blood, and His name is called the Word of God. And the armies of heaven, clothed in fine linen, white and clean, followed Him on white horses. Now out of His mouth goes a sharp sword, that with it He should strike the nations. And He Himself will rule them with a rod of iron. He Himself treads the winepress of the fierceness and wrath of Almighty God. And He has on His robe and on His thigh a name written: KING OF KINGS AND LORD OF LORDS."*

When Jesus left earth after commissioning His disciples to proclaim the Gospel to all nations, He left from Mt. Olives. As the disciples watched Him go, the angels spoke to them. They said to them, as recorded in Acts 1:11, that in the same way they saw Jesus leave He will also come again. When Jesus returns to earth it will be to that same place, Mt. Olives. Zechariah 14:1-7 describes the return. As Jesus lands on earth, Mt. Olives is split in half and the ground to the temple site is leveled. Thus on level ground Jesus marches in to conquer and establish His kingdom on earth. He destroys the armies of the Antichrist with His Word. The Antichrist himself and the leader of the false church are cast alive into hell. Satan is bound, and a new order of living begins on earth.

In the next chapter we will see how Jesus reigns on earth for a thousand years, before the final judgment and the new heaven and earth come. How encouraging it is for those who have committed their lives to Jesus Christ as Messiah, Savior, Lord, and King, to know how certain the end is. What boldness they can have as they live. What peace they can have as they anticipate the future. All that God has decreed will come to pass. It will come to pass in our generation. It will come to pass in your lifetime. How important it is to ensure that your allegiance to the Lord Jesus Christ, is the clear and compelling purpose of your life.

# 23 | The Day of Righteousness

*"And the Lord shall be King over all the earth. In that day it shall be—"The Lord is one, and His name one."*
Zechariah 14:9

**W**hen God makes a promise you can write it down, it is guaranteed, it will come to pass. Back some eighteen hundred years before Jesus was born amongst us, God had made a promise to a man named Abraham. He made a promise that one day from his seed would come a man who would rule the nations of the world from the land that God had promised to Abraham. Some eight hundred years later under the leadership of the second King of Israel, David, Israel came as close as it has come to the fulfillment of this promise. David, taking Israel to the height of its power, only occupied 10% of the land that had been promised to Abraham. God added to the promise when He sent word to David that He would one day bring from the seed of David a King, who would bring in an everlasting kingdom of righteousness. God told David, as recorded in 2 Samuel 7:16, *"And your house and your kingdom shall be established forever before you. Your throne shall be established forever."* In all the years since, God has never fulfilled that promise. But God is faithful, what He has said He will do. As we learned in Romans 11:29, *"For the gifts and the calling of God are irrevocable."*

When Jesus comes back to earth to end the Tribulation, He comes to stay. He comes to stay and rule for a thousand years. Revelation 20:1-6 gives a very sparse description of these thousand years. Why such extensive description of seven years, and such a sparse description of the next one thousand years? The reason for the sparse description of the next one thousand years, is that those who belong to God will no longer be living by faith. The Bible says the saints will live in the presence of Jesus in Jerusalem. They have been resurrected, they have been glorified, they have been perfected in their likeness to Christ. No longer living by the promises, they will now live in the fulfillment of the promises.

As Jesus comes back to earth the Tribulation saints are resurrected into the likeness of Jesus, the Old Testament saints as well having been added to the resurrected church, the bride of Christ. All of these have passed into the new and eternal order for the saints. No more presence of sin, no more bodies subject to pain, disease, death. They are now as they will gloriously ever be. What Revelation 20:6 describes as the first Ressurection is complete. They are now on earth to join in the thousand-year rule of the Lord Jesus Christ over the nations of the world. Satan is bound and no longer has freedom to work through mankind in rebellion against God and His rule.

The home of the resurrected saints for the thousand years, is their eternal home, the new Jerusalem. Already in heaven God has built the new Jerusalem. A place has been built for every saint. It is their eternal home. Jesus talked in the beginning of John 14 about His going to heaven to prepare a place for all those who have committed their lives to Him as Messiah, Savior and Lord. This new Jerusalem comes to earth after the Tribulation. Ezekiel 40-47 describes the focal point of this new Jerusalem, a glorious Temple for the worship of God. Revelation 21 describes the new Jerusalem in its dimensions and features. It is huge, about 1800 miles in width and length.

But who does Jesus rule over? It is obvious from the Bible that not all peoples and nations are destroyed in the judgments and battle of Armageddon. Many people survive. It seems that there are some nations that have not fully participated in the worship of the Antichrist, and in the persecution of those who bear the Name of Jesus. There are some who have offered refuge, shelter, clothing, food. It is they who are mentioned in Matthew 25:31-46. These nations gain favor as Jesus has now come to rule.

Of course the world is in horrible condition at the end of the Tribulation. The judgments of God and the consequences of the nuclear warfare used have all but ruined life on earth. As Jesus comes He comes with healing to the earth. There are some practical matters that need to be attended to. Ezekiel 39 indicates that it takes seven years just to gather and burn the weapons of war in Israel. It will take seven months to bury the dead. Some of them are marked, indicating a likelihood of nuclear radiation that makes them too 'hot' to be handled.

As the new Jerusalem is described, it tells of a river that flows from the throne of God through it going out the gates to Jerusalem and there are trees beside the river. As the water flows out from Jerusalem into the sea, the water brings healing to the seas. Listen to how Ezekiel describes this in Ezekiel 47:8-12, " . . . *This water flows toward the eastern region, goes down into the valley, and enters the sea. When it reaches the sea, its waters are healed. . . . There will be a very great multitude of fish, because these waters go there; for they will be healed, and everything will live wherever the river goes . . . . Along the banks of the river, on this side and that, will grow all kinds of trees used for food; their leaves will not wither, and their fruit will not fail. They will bear fruit every month, because their water flows from the sanctuary. Their fruit will be for food, and their leaves for medicine.*" How wonderful and gracious God is, as Jesus rules the nations it is with blessing to all. The waters are healed. The fish renew. The trees along the river bear monthly fruit given to the nations for food. Because those outside the city are not the saints, they are still subject to the consequences of sin. Sickness and disease are still part of their lives. But the leaves from the trees along the River of Life are used for healing.

While the peoples outside Jerusalem are still subject to the curse, sickness, disease, and death, it seems that Jesus returns the earth to in some ways what it was like before the flood of Noah's day. Life expectancy, for example, dramatically changes. The Bible says that someone who dies at a hundred will seem to have died as a baby. The effect of the curse in the animal world changes. All animals become grass eaters. Isaiah 11:6-9, *"The wolf also shall dwell with the lamb, the leopard shall lie down with the young goat, the calf and the young lion and the fatling to-gether; and the little child shall lead them. The cow and the bear shall graze; their young ones shall lie down together; and the lion shall eat straw like the ox. The nursing child shall play by the cobra's hole, and the weaned child shall put his hand in the viper's den. They shall not hurt nor destroy in all My holy mountain, for the earth shall be full of the knowledge of the Lord as the waters cover the sea."*

When Jesus reigns on earth, the Bible promises there will be justice. The rights of the poor will be protected. Those who would break the law will find that justice is swift, perfect, and final. Isaiah 2:4 says that no longer will people be making weapons of war, but they will be making work tools, *" . . . They shall beat their swords into plowshares, and their spears into pruning hooks; nation shall not lift up sword against nation, neither shall they learn war anymore."* All the best of what mankind has longed for will be achieved. The longing for a world of peace, prosperity, justice, and security will come through the rule of Jesus and the upholding of His law and ways.

The nations of the world will be required to come and to honor Jesus as Lord and King in worship. Zechariah 14:16-17 describes how this happens, and the encouragement the nations will have to do it, *"And it shall come to pass that everyone who is*

*left of all the nations which came against Jerusalem shall go up
from year to year to worship the King, the Lord of hosts, and to
keep the Feast of Tabernacles. And it shall be that whichever of the
families of the earth do not come up to Jerusalem to worship the
King, the Lord of hosts, on them there will be no rain."* Thus, the
withholding of rain will be the encouragement to come to Jerusalem to worship. The Feast of the Tabernacles is the last of the
Feasts given to Israel. It is the feast of the harvest, the ingather-
ing of all with which God has blessed the land. Jesus enjoying
for a thousand years the harvest of His work, the fulfillment of
the promises to rule over the nations.

While representatives of the nations of the world come to
Jerusalem, they are not allowed to enter. Only the redeemed of
the Lord have the right of entrance to the new Jerusalem. They
alone have the right to the tree of life. Outside the city are the
unredeemed. That is what Revelation describes in 21:27, and in
22:14-15, *"But there shall by no means enter it anything that
defiles, or causes an abomination or a lie, but only those who are
written in the Lamb's book of life . . . . Blessed are those who do
His commandments, that they may have the right to the tree of
life, and may enter through the gates into the city. But outside are
dogs and sorcerers and sexually immoral and murderers and idolaters, and whoever loves and practices a lie."*

You would think that a world that knew the perfect rule of the
Lord Jesus Christ for a thousand years would want to serve and
honor Him out of a devoted heart. You would think that seeing
the blessings that come to life and the world when Jesus rules,
having been seen for a thousand years, would find people wanting them to never end. You would think that, but you would be
wrong. For after a thousand years, Satan who has been bound, is
loosed. Once more he can go among people and work. Once
more he can offer the lie, that people themselves can be gods.
Once more he incites them that good is bad, and evil is good.
People quickly turn on the living God, and the nations of the
world march once again in war. Revelation 20:7-10 describes

them marching against the new Jerusalem from every direction. There is no real battle, though. Revelation simply says that fire comes down from heaven and destroys them all. The Devil is taken to be thrown finally and eternally into hell.

The end of the thousand years portrays what has been mankind's problem from the beginning. The problem is that our hearts are in rebellion against God. The only answer to the problem of the heart is a heart transforming salvation by faith in the Lord Jesus Christ, His Cross, and Ressurection triumph. Even in a perfect world, seeing the rule of Jesus firsthand, people still reject Him. There is no evidence that people are saved during those thousand years. They worshiped Jesus only from the outside, not from the heart. Only the miraculous work of God through the Gospel of the Lord Jesus Christ can really change people. Our problems at their core are not genetic, environmental, educational, financial, social, or political. Sin comes from the heart, and the heart is rebellious. Make sure your heart is hearing and responding to the call of God to salvation by faith in the Lord Jesus Christ. There is salvation in no other name. There is hope in no other name. May the message of this truth bring you to the worship, love, honor, trust, obedience to the Lord Jesus Christ as your personal Messiah, Savior, and Lord.

# 24 | The Day of Judgment and

# New Beginning

*"And I heard a loud voice from heaven saying, "Behold the tabernacle of God is with men, and He will dwell with them, and they shall be His people. God Himself will be with them and be their God."* . . . *But the cowardly, unbelieving, abominable, murderers, sexually immoral, sorcerers, idolaters, and all liars shall have their part in the lake which burns with fire and brimstone, which is the second death."*
Revelation 21:3,8

Eternity, it thrills me, scares me, overwhelms me, calls me. The Bible says God has set eternity in each of our hearts (Ecclesiastes 3:11). Eternity is rooted in the very existence of God. God has no beginning and He will have no end. He is the great "I Am." We know logically this must be true. Something, someone has no beginning. To the materialists, it is matter. But by the revelation of God, through the Bible, His written Word, and through His Son, the Lord Jesus Christ, His living Word, God is the eternal One. He is the cause of all that is. As God is the "I Am," with no beginning, He will also have no end. This God has made man to share in His likeness. He has created him with a soul, the core of his being is spiritual.

While man has beginning, as a creation of God, he has no ending. All of us will live, exist forever. The Bible teaches that all of us, each of us, will be resurrected in a new body that will never be destroyed. Our new bodies will be immortal. While all of us will live forever, there is as big a difference between where and how we will live forever as one could imagine. In fact the reality of eternity is beyond our imagination.

As the rule of Jesus for a thousand year ends in the rebellion and defeat of the nations, inspired and led by Satan, time as we know it ends. What began in the Garden of Eden has now been completed. What started with sin and the curse has now been resolved by Jesus, through the Cross, Ressurection, and return to reign for a thousand years. The promises to Abraham, and those who followed of what God would do in and through the nation of Israel have all been fulfilled. The Feasts of Israel have each been fulfilled by the Lord Jesus Christ. It is the end of what for us has been the beginning. For the end of the thousand years introduces what for mankind will be the beginning of eternity. The entering of an eternal condition that will never change. How wise are those people who today live in the moment with the clear focus on the reality of eternity never forgotten. How foolish are those people today who live in the moment with no clear focus on the reality of eternity.

The first action as time ends is the one long awaited by the saints. Satan is cast into hell forever. He does not pass go, he does not collect $200.00, he goes directly to hell and he enters a place that has no exit. What is hell? What is this place in which so many will exist forever? The Bible has a surprising amount to say about hell. In fact it has more to say in volume about hell than it does about heaven. God wants us to know of hell's reality so that we will know and understand the consequences of our choices today.

Hell is a place. It is real. It exists today. Hell has been prepared by God as a place of eternal judgment. It is a place of eternal judgment, not originally prepared for man, but for Satan and the approximately one third of the angels who followed him in rebellion against God. As we learned, this happened before mankind and this heaven and earth as we know it was shaped. When Satan and the angels rebelled, God prepared a place of judgment for them. That place of judgment is hell. Matthew 25:41 states that truth clearly, *"Then He will also say to those on the left hand, "Depart from Me, you cursed, into the everlasting fire prepared for the devil and his angels."*

The Bible gives us a lot of word pictures concerning hell that are descriptive, horrifying, terrifying. They are never presented as exaggeration or pretend, they are given with frank honesty. They are given to warn the wicked of the consequences of their ways. They are given to encourage the saints that their longing for judgment will be fulfilled. The very word used for hell in the Bible had an image for the people of that day that was powerful. The word is for a place called Gehenna in a valley in the land of Israel called Hinnom. In Israel's history it was a place where pagans practiced human sacrifice, but it also served a more practical purpose. It became a trash site for garbage, rubbish. The rubbish was burned there in fires that continually smoldered. Thus the picture of a place of waste where the fire is always burning, smoldering, was a very real one in everyone's mind of what the Bible warns of when it describes hell. God never wants hell to be an abstract, distant concept, but real and motivating. He wants it to be a place we say, "I never want to be there!"

There are numerous other descriptions of hell. It is called a lake of fire (Revelation 20:10). Jesus used powerful pictures of it from the Old Testament, when He describes it as a place, *"where, 'Their worm does not die, and the fire is not quenched.'" (Mark 9:48).* Worms feed on the dead and decayed. But in this case it never ends. Fire normally consumes what it burns, but in hell it never consumes, it goes on and on. Hell is described as a bottomless pit (Revelation 20:3). Like a dream you might have had that you were falling with nothing to catch you, so is hell as a bottomless pit into which one is thrown. It is called a place of utter darkness, in which no light is ever seen (Matthew 8:12). It is called a place of torment (Revelation 20:10). It is called a place where people are continually weeping, wailing, gnashing their teeth (Matthew 8:12). It is called a place where angels and people will be assigned for eternity. It has no end. It has no exits. It is called the second death (Revelation 20:14). Death in the sense of separation from God, Who is life. God warned the soul that sinners will die, be separated from Him Who is life. The second death is for those who have lived and died without calling upon God's salvation through the Lord Jesus Christ.

The assignment to hell will be one rooted in justice. God has a judicial anger and wrath against sin. Sin perverts, robs, ruins, destroys. Sin is personal against God, in that it is an act against God and His right to rule. Sin is personal acts against God's creation. Sin is personal acts against people that have been made in the image of God. Sin is a personal act against self, who has been made in the image of God. Sin is the all we should have done, but didn't. All of the person and character of God reacts against sin. The true marvel of the ages is not that God has set a date for judgment, and a place for judgment. The true wonder is that God has restrained His wrath and saved it for the day when justice will be served. It is the wonder of God's restraint that led the prophet Jeremiah to say in Lamentations 3:22, *"Through the Lord's mercies we are not consumed, because His compassions fail not."* But while the day of justice may seem to us delayed, it is certain and it will be terrifying in a terror that will never end.

The Bible indicates that all judgment for mankind has been given to the Lord Jesus Christ. After the thousand-year reign on earth, the Day of Judgment for mankind without saving faith in the Lord Jesus Christ comes. The face of Jesus when He comes in judgment is so fierce that the Bible portrays heaven and earth fleeing from the terror of His presence. Revelation 20:11 puts it this way, *"Then I saw a great white throne and Him who sat on it, from whose face the earth and the heaven fled away. And there was found no place for them."* Certainly a different picture of Jesus than too many carry in their mind.

At the end, as Jesus comes to judge, all of those who have lived and died without saving faith in the Lord Jesus Christ are resurrected. They receive an immortal body. It is not described but it is certain that it does not share in the likeness of the glory of the Lord Jesus Christ. But it is real, and what it experiences is real. After resurrection each person, one by one, all alone, comes into the courtroom. No one escapes the judgment. Rich and poor, great and small, all are resurrected to face that day. The Bible, when talking about this, mentions that the sea gives up its dead, as well as death and Hades. It isn't that there are different categories of dead, or places they are kept. There were many in that day that felt if there was no body, there would be no resurrection. The great fear was to die at sea and your body lost to the elements. It was feared that they would never have a resurrection. Thus the Bible is addressing that fear directly and saying that the sea gave up their dead. It is no problem for God to resurrect whether the person died at sea, was cremated, or had their body sent into space.

Where have those who have died been prior to judgment? The Bible teaches that those who die without saving faith in the Lord Jesus Christ have spent the 'in between' time from their death until Judgement Day, in a place called Hades. Hades is a real place. It is a place of torment. The wicked have no rest in death. Jesus referred to Hades in a parable He told. He pictured a man who was there as being in torment (Luke 16:22). Hades is not hell the place, but it may well seem like it. Those who are there are kept for the Day of Judgment, and their final place of eternal confinement. It is like a person accused of a serious crime who is held without bail in the city or county jail. It isn't prison where they will be sent if found guilty, but it has great similarity.

When a person comes to court, they will find that a book has been kept on them. In the books are recorded all the thoughts, words, deeds, actions of their life. The books record not only the deed, but the motivation behind the act. Each deed is measured against the standard of righteousness. God has established what is right and what is wrong. It is a standard that is not only right, it is beautiful. For God's holiness, righteousness, standard, is the perfection of love. Holy love fulfills all of God's requirements. He asks only that we love Him with all our heart, soul, mind, and strength, and that we love our neighbor in a way that treats them with the love we would want if we were in their place. All of our acts are judged against that standard. If we fall short, than we are inexcusably guilty before God. There is no justification for sin. Every act of sin is an act of rebellion against God, and His right to rule. The Bible calls sin lawlessness. A spirit that rejects God and His right to rule. The Bible says if a person breaks even one part of the law that may not be its most significant, that person is still as guilty as one who has repeatedly broken it all. It is all rebellion against God, an inexcusable act of treason. The reality the Bible gives us is that we all sin repeatedly. We fall short of the standard of God's glory and perfection every day of our lives.

Each person will be found guilty. Each will have a day in court, but they will have no defense. Each will hear the sentence of condemnation and the assignment to hell. There is no second chance to reconsider a commitment to the Lord Jesus Christ. The Bible teaches that it is given to man once to die, and then comes the judgment (Hebrews 9:27) The length of the term is eternity. This is a separation that can never be bridged. It is a body in which the worm will never turn nor the fire ever be quenched. This is the second death. Death being separation from God, and the second death is permanent. While all the guilty will be consigned to hell the Bible indicates that there are degrees of punishment. Jesus teaches this as recorded in Luke 12:47-48, *"And that servant who knew His master's will, and did not prepare himself or do according to his will, shall be beaten with many stripes. But he who did not know, yet committed things deserving of stripes, shall be beaten with few. For everyone to whom much is given, from him much will be required; and to whom much has been committed, of him they will ask the more."* In this case the degree of punishment is related to amount of knowledge, and what one did with what one knows. While ignorance of the law does not lead to forgiveness, it does lead to less severity in judgment, than one who knew and deliberately broke the law anyway. Jesus also indicates in other places that those who teach bear a greater responsibility in judgment. And, an even greater judgment is for those who would sin against children, or lead children into sin.

What a terrifying reality hell is. How important it is that we turn from sin to the open arms and amazing grace of God in the Lord Jesus Christ. How sobering it is to realize that many people who consider themselves Christians will be sent to hell. Jesus describes many who are amazed that they are going to hell. Jesus says of them in Matthew 7:21-23, *"Not everyone who says to me, 'Lord, Lord,' shall enter the kingdom of heaven, but he who does the will of My Father in heaven. Many will say to Me in that day, "Lord, Lord, have we not prophesied in Your name, cast out demons in Your name, and done many wonders in Your name?' And then I will declare to them, 'I never knew you; depart from Me, you who practice lawlessness!'"* Jesus is saying that being a Christian is not just a matter of what a person says, it is a new direction in life that is reflected in what a person does. Jesus says they still practice lawlessness. They have never really submitted their will to the Lordship of Jesus Christ. Make sure your heart is truly submitted to Him. How awful it will be to find oneself in hell, and know there is no escape, to understand there will be no end.

The Bible indicates, in contrast to the wicked, those who have lived with saving faith in the Lord Jesus Christ will never face a judgment for sin. Their Day of Judgment for sin was faced by the Lord Jesus Christ on the Cross almost two thousand years ago. Justice has been done. They have not been forgiven because God is loving and kind. They are forgiven because Jesus satisfied the wrath of God against their sin on the Cross. Sin only has to be paid for once, and as we have learned, Jesus paid once for all who will put their trust in Him. Romans 8:1 gives the thrilling results, there is no condemnation, no guilty judgment for those who are in Christ Jesus. Praise God. His forgiveness through the blood of Jesus is complete, and eternal.

While the Christian will never face a day of judgment for sin, they will face a day of reward or loss for their works as Christians. At some point, before the end of the seven years of the Tribulation, each believer will face a day of evaluation before the Lord. What will be judged is their faithfulness as stewards of the gifts and resources that God has entrusted to them. A Christian is never judged for the results of a life, for results are the work of the Holy Spirit. A Christian is only judged on the basis of faithfulness. Paul describes this judgment and its motivating force in his life this way in 1 Corinthians 3:11-15, *"For no other foundation can anyone lay than that which is laid, which is Jesus Christ. Now if anyone builds on this foundation with gold, silver, precious stones, wood, hay, straw, each one's work will become clear; for that Day will declare it, because it will be revealed by fire; and the fire will test each one's work, of what sort it is. If anyone's work which he built on it endures, he will receive a reward. If anyone's work is burned, he will suffer loss; but he himself will be saved, yet so as through fire."*

The Bible indicates that just as there are degrees of punishment in hell, so there are degrees of reward in heaven. One evidence of reward will be crowns that are given. These are not crowns of rulers, but crowns of honor. Another way the faithful will be rewarded is with increased responsibilities in service to the Lord in eternity. In eternity the saints will be active, busy, productive. The Bible states in 1 Corinthians 6 that part of the responsibilities in eternity will be ruling over angels. We share with Christ in His role as King, not just in the millennium, but for eternity. Jesus in Matthew 25 through the teaching of the parable of the talents, indicates the reward for faithfulness will be increased responsibilities in serving Him. Matthew 25:23 gives teaching on this aspect of eternal reward, *"His lord said to him, 'Well done, good and faithful servant; you have been faithful over a few things, I will make you ruler over many things. Enter into the joy of your Lord."*

At this end of the thousand-year reign of Christ, this earth is consumed with fire. This earth is destroyed. All of creation is not destroyed, just this heaven and earth. A new heaven and earth is created. Every indication is that it will be very much like this one, only no longer with any curse upon it because of sin. God loves this heaven and earth He created. He delighted in it at creation. He saw all that He had made was good and He took pleasure in it. He will also delight in creating the new heaven and earth. The new Jerusalem that has come down from the third heaven, where God is now, has been removed from the earth while it was destroyed. It then comes down to the new heaven and earth, where it will be for eternity.

The real wonder of the new heaven and earth, and eternity, will not be the wonder of the new world. No more sin, sickness, death, pain, separation. The real wonder of heaven is that God will make His permanent dwelling place with us. The marvel of eternity is not that man gets to go to heaven and be with God, it is that God comes to earth to make His dwelling place with man. Listen again to Revelation 21:3, *"And I heard a loud voice from heaven saying, 'Behold the tabernacle of God is with men, and He will dwell with them, and they shall be His people. God Himself will be with them, and be their God."*

Will you be part of this? Which of these two eternal destinies will be yours? In this next chapter we will share with you this last time, how to have peace with God. How to have your sins forgiven. How to respond to God's amazing free gift of salvation through saving faith in the Lord Jesus Christ. Be sure about this, for the consequences are eternal.

# 25 | The Day to Choose

*"And the Spirit and the bride says, 'Come!' And let him who hears say, 'Come'! And let him who thirsts come. Whoever desires, let him take the water of life freely."*
Revelation 22:17

We have learned all of the key points of the story of our generation, the culmination of history, the return of the Lord Jesus Christ as King of Kings, and Lord of Lords, the final judgment and reward. We have learned all of the key elements of the story, but one. The one part yet to be certain about is yours. Where will you spend eternity? Are you sure? I'd like to share with you again how you can be saved from this judgment that is coming, and be at peace with God now and for eternity. Nothing could be more important.

As we come to the end of the book of Revelation, it gives a passionate plea to all who hear to come to God through the Lord Jesus Christ. It portrays the Spirit (the Holy Spirit) and the bride (the church) bringing a single passionate message to the world, come receive the free gift of salvation. Let me encourage you as you read this, if you feel the desire in your heart to be saved, it is not too late for you. But you must act, and you must act now. Even if you are reading this while the Tribulation is going on, it is not too late for you. Maybe a loved one has witnessed to you, left you this book. It is a gift from God, and it comes with a shout of hope. It is not too late, choose this day the Lord Jesus Christ.

Embrace Him, trust Him, obey Him, follow Him, stand for Him, never deny Him. How can you do that? Let me tell you briefly from the words of Jesus how to do that. Listen for the Spirit of God to speak to you as you read.

Jesus presented the issue of salvation very clearly in a phrase that has become quite popularly used and misused in our culture. Jesus says, *"Most assuredly, I say to you, unless one is born again, he cannot see the kingdom of God . . . . Do not marvel that I said to you, 'You must be born again.'"*, John 3:3,5. Jesus says to you, you must be born again. The word again can also be understood to mean above. Jesus is referring to the truth that a new birth into the kingdom of God comes by the work and power of the Holy Spirit. You cannot change yourself. You can only want to be changed. The new birth, the transformation comes from God, it is not something you or anybody else can produce. How can one be born spiritually into the kingdom of God? How can one be born by the Holy Spirit? There is great, good news. This new birth comes as a gift to all who will call upon God through the Lord Jesus Christ. How can you do this? Let's see the simple explanation that Jesus gives as to how one can be born again from above by God.

Jesus says first in John 3:13, that understanding that Jesus alone is the only way of salvation is the first truth, *"No one has ascended to heaven but He who came down from heaven, that is, the Son of Man who is in heaven."* Jesus clearly states that no one on their own has made it to heaven. No one has ascended to heaven. The only way salvation is possible is by the Lord Jesus Christ, the Son of Man, who came from heaven to be born among us. Salvation is possible by Jesus alone.

In this truth is something I must know about myself, and something I must know about Jesus. I must know about myself that I cannot make it to heaven based on who I am, or by good works that I do to make me good enough. The Bible says that all of us are like sheep. We have gone astray. We have each gone our own way. We have not loved the Lord our God with all our heart, soul, mind, and strength. We have not always loved our neighbor as ourselves. That is sin. It is a rebellion against God. We are without excuse. We are without remedy by ourselves, or in any religion or religious act. No one has ascended into heaven.

In this truth I must also recognize who Jesus is. He is the One who is in heaven, who came to earth. I must understand the uniqueness of Jesus. He is God Himself. God who is one, exists in three distinct persons, Father, Son, and Holy Spirit. Jesus was sent by the Father to be born amongst us. He is God who became man. He never stopped being God, but He did set aside His glory, and made Himself like us in every way, except He did not sin. No sin was in Jesus. God sent Jesus into the world to be our Savior and to lead us to a saving relationship with God that will last for eternity. No one on their own has ever ascended to heaven. Salvation comes by Jesus alone, who came down from heaven.

The second truth Jesus gives is that salvation comes by the Cross of Jesus alone. He says in John 3:14, *"And as Moses lifted up the serpent in the wilderness, even so must the Son of Man be lifted up."* In this truth Jesus calls upon an incident recorded in the Old Testament in Numbers 21 to explain the meaning and the power of His Cross. The people of Israel were being led in the wilderness toward the promised land by Moses. The people though complained against God and Moses. They said it would have been better to have been left in slavery in Egypt. God began to judge the people for their rebellion by sending fiery serpents into their midst. Whoever the serpents bit died. The people recognized this as the judgment of God. They went to Moses and begged him to intercede with God on their behalf. They were sorry for their sins and complaints. God heard their cry and offered them a path of forgiveness. He ordered Moses to make a brass image of a fiery serpent. He told him to put it on a staff and hold it up high. God told Moses to tell the people to be saved from the poison of the fiery serpent all they had to do is to look at the serpent held up high by Moses. Even if they were bitten, if they would just look upon the serpent they would be saved.

In this incident God was giving a picture of Jesus and the Cross. Just as the serpent was lifted up high to save guilty people, so would Jesus be lifted up on the Cross so that guilty sinners can be saved from the judgment of God they deserve. Jesus died on the Cross in judgment as a substitute for us. He paid for sin in full. As we have learned, He did not stay dead, but on the third day He rose victorious from the grave. Salvation comes for you, when you look upon Jesus and what He did on the Cross as the gift of salvation for you. Salvation comes by the Cross of Jesus alone.

The third truth Jesus gives for how one can be born again is the key one, for it is the action step. Jesus teaches that salvation comes by faith alone. He says in John 3:15, *"that whoever believes in Him should not perish but have eternal life."* Jesus says salvation comes by believing, meaning by faith. Believing is a powerful action word that is not well understood by many. When we think of believing, we think of agreement. We think of it as an intellectual issue. But believing is not an intellectual agreement, oh it is that, I understand and agree with the truth. Believing is built on the foundation of commitment to the truth. Faith though is a powerful action word that expresses a whole continuing direction of life.

What does it mean to believe? I find a story from a traveling circus at the beginning of the 20th century helpful in understanding. As the circus came to a town it would put on a show at noon on main street of whatever town it was in. One feature would be a high wire strung across the street. The high wire performer was quite a showman who engaged the crowd. As they watched, he would cry out, "How many of you believe I can safely walk across this wire and back?" The crowd would enthusiastically say, "We believe you can do that." And he would walk safely back and forth. Up there with him he had a wheel barrow with a grooved wheel. He would ask the crowd, "How many of you believe I can safely wheel this barrow across the wire and back?" Again the crowd would enthusiastically call out, "We believe you can do that." And he would safely wheel the barrow across and back. Then he would say, "How many of you believe I could safely wheel this barrow across and back with somebody in it?" By now convinced of his skill, they would enthusiastically call out, "We believe you can do that." He would then call back to the crowd, "OK, who will get in and let me prove it?" It is in this action that we see the true definition of faith as Jesus used it. It is not faith when you stand on the ground and believe that he could safely wheel you across the wire and back in a barrow. It is only faith as Jesus uses it, when you leave the crowd, climb in the barrow, and trust the one to wheel you safely across and back.

What does it mean to believe in Jesus? It is faith that what He has done on the Cross is totally enough to satisfy God's judgment for your sin. It is to totally trust that by receiving the gift of salvation you will be saved from God's judgment. It is to believe that Jesus conquered death and rose from the grave. It is to have the hope in His Ressurection, and in His Ressurection power to change your life.

Faith also is a commitment to follow Jesus in obedience and trust. It is a commitment to a new and lasting direction in your life. You leave the crowd to believe in and follow Jesus. You leave the lifestyles choices of sin. No one does this perfectly. It is not that you never sin again. It is that you don't want to sin, and you commit to walk following Jesus and His way for your life. That means you want to know the Bible and what it says about how a Christian lives. You are serious about a commitment to follow Jesus.

When the Bible describes in Revelation 12:11 those who are saved, it gives three characteristics of their lives, *"And they over-came him by the blood of the Lamb and by the word of their testimony, and they did not love their lives to the death."* The first characteristic is that they put their whole trust in the blood of Jesus for the forgiveness of their sins. The second characteristic is that they were not ashamed of the Name of Jesus. They pub-licly identified themselves as believers in Jesus Christ. The third characteristic is that they would not give up their faith in Jesus even if it meant imprisonment or death.

If you are reading this in parts of the world that are hostile to the Gospel of Jesus, or if you are reading this during the Tribulation you must understand the possible price for following Jesus. As we have seen, Revelation clearly says that some of you will go to prison, and some of you will be put to death (Revelation 13:9,10; 14:12-13). Whatever you do, do not deny the Name of Jesus and do not take the mark of the Beast. Your pain and trouble will be short, and God will help you through it, and your reward will be eternal. Read Revelation, it is God's survival guide for you.

Ready to take the step of commitment to Jesus? It is life's most important step. Let me give you a simple prayer that if you understand and pray believing what you say, then you can know God has saved you. Prayer is simply talking to God. He is present everywhere. He can hear your words, whether they are in your heart or audibly by your voice. Simply pray this as a model prayer, *"Dear God, I know that I am a sinner. I am sorry for my sins. I believe that Jesus died on the Cross as a payment for my sins. I believe He rose again from the grave. I believe that salvation is a gift to all who call upon Jesus. I call upon Jesus right now. Forgive my sins. Come into my life to be my Savior and Lord. I make a promise to You, with Your help, as best I can, I will follow You for the rest of my life. Thank You for saving me. Amen."*

Prayed that? Believed that? Than you are saved. You may not feel different, but you have taken God at His word and acted, and He has promised that you are saved. Emotions, feelings will follow. What is important is that you now live out your new life. Begin talking to God, that is prayer. Begin listening to God by reading the Bible and asking Him to speak to you about it. Obey what it commands you, trust what it promises you. Find other Christians and begin to worship God together. Share with others the Good News of how God has saved you, and how He wants to save them.

May God bless you in your new walk in Jesus, and may God keep you safe from the judgment that is coming. Let me close with a benediction and promise from God's Word as given Jude 24-25, *"Now to Him who is able to keep you from stumbling, and to present you faultless before the presence of His glory with exceeding joy, to God our Savior, Who alone is wise, be glory and majesty, dominion and power, both now and forever. Amen."*